BERKSHIRE'S
MILITARY HERITAGE

Dean Hollands

AMBERLEY

This book is dedicated to the memory of all those whose actions and deeds have created Berkshire's military heritage, and to those who continue to preserve it.

First published 2023

Amberley Publishing
The Hill, Stroud
Gloucestershire, GL5 4EP

www.amberley-books.com

Copyright © Dean Hollands, 2023

Logo source material courtesy of Gerry van Tonder

The right of Dean Hollands to be identified as the Author of this work has been asserted in accordance with the Copyrights, Designs and Patents Act 1988.

ISBN 978 1 3981 0924 7 (print)
ISBN 978 1 3981 0925 4 (ebook)

British Library Cataloguing in Publication Data.
A catalogue record for this book is available from the British Library.

Typesetting by SJmagic DESIGN SERVICES, India.
Printed in Great Britain.

Contents

Introduction

Berkshire has an ancient military history, the heritage of which reflects the diversity of the people, places and events that created it. For centuries invaders, raiders and conquering armies have stained its soil red with their blood battling, building and bruising their way across the county's historic landscape. A landscape that has witnessed kingdoms rise and fall and their boundaries form, expand and contract.

From hill forts and fortified towns to Norman castles and nuclear bunkers, throughout history Berkshire's defences have repelled aggressors and provided deterrents against the threat of tyranny, and terrorism at home and overseas. Its airfields have defended the nation's airspace and supported major military conflicts around the world throughout the twentieth century.

Berkshire's military links to the English Civil, Crimean and Boer wars are commemorated, as are the deeds of its soldiers and civilians during both world wars. Men and women from many nations lost their lives bravely defending the county during the Second World War. Others lost their lives in tragic circumstances, unwitting victims and unsung heroes who are remembered on monuments and memorials across the county.

The extensive nature of Berkshire's military heritage is truly amazing. Such is the scale of the heritage to be found, it is not possible to comment in depth on any aspect in this publication. Rather, this book offers a concise and informative overview of the important periods in the county's military history and some of the many personalities and events that have created its remarkable military legacy.

In so doing the book signposts readers to key heritage attractions and locations to be found within the county's modern and former boundaries and celebrates the lives, stories, and achievements of those who have through word and deed shaped it. Berkshire has a rich and proud military heritage, and it is the author's hope that readers will be inspired and stimulated to learn more about the county's military history and explore further the many wonderful military heritage attractions and sites it offers.

1. Invasion and Occupation

When the last dry 'land bridge' connecting Britain to mainland Europe collapsed around 8200 BCE, the nomadic migrations of Stone Age people into Britain ceased. The first of a long line of invaders were Bronze Age explorers in search of fertile lands, minerals, and other valuable resources. Germany was the last nation to attempt an invasion during the 1940s, but before them the county experienced a stream of invaders, raiders, and conquerors. Roman legions, Germanic hoards, Danish Vikings, and an army of men made up of Normans, Bretons, Flemish, and men from other French provinces, have all shaped and influenced the county's military heritage.

The Romans invaded Britain in CE 43 at the instigation of King Verica of the Atrebates, a Celtic tribe originally from Gaul. In CE 40, King Cunobelinus conquered the Atrebate kingdom and ousted King Verica to become 'Britannorum Rex', king of the Britons.

In response, Emperor Claudius used this request as an opportunity to make a military name for himself and, having secured justification from the Senate to invade Britain, left with a force of 40,000 soldiers headed by General Aulus Plautius. The main invasion force arrived in southern Britain and spent the first few years battling its bloody way inland. Conquering and subjugating tribes who opposed them, Plautius' forces executed an unrelenting and aggressive style of attack, storming defensive settlements, ransacking villages, destroying crops, and stealing livestock and other resources.

Re-enactors, Legio VIII Augusta MGV.

Re-enactors, Legio VIII
Augusta MGV.

Unlike the invasion and occupations of Kent, Sussex and Hampshire, the Roman army's engagement with Berkshire was a more amenable affair. Plautius restored Vericus' kingdom to him when the Second Roman Augustan Legion, commanded by General Vespasian, arrived at Chichester in CE 49. Rome's invasion of their ally the Atrebates' territory, which included modern Berkshire, was peaceful, allowing the Atrebates to prosper. Some tribes submitted, others refused, and subjugating Britain took another forty-four years. During this time, the Romans occupied and refortified the main hill forts of their allies and those they had conquered.

However, Rome's aggressive empire building could not last forever, and by CE 388 the Roman empire was falling apart. With barbarian attacks on Rome, Emperor Honorius recalled his legions from Britain. During CE 410, the Romans left Britain to itself and the country fell into chaos. Towns fell into disrepair and people returned to the countryside, living in farmsteads and roundhouses, surrounded by small defensive embankments. Britain was soon under continuous attack: native tribes battled among themselves, against the Picts in the north, the Irish in the west and European invaders in the east and south, all desperate to fill the power vacuum left by the Romans.

During the fifth century, Vortigern, king of the Britons, enlisted a mercenary army, which included Angles, Saxons, Batavians, Franks, Frisians and Jutes – powerful warlike tribes from Germany and Southern Scandinavia. Vortigern promised land in return for fighting the Picts and Scots, but the Anglo-Saxons invited more of their countrymen to join them and subsequently demanded more land provisions. At a meeting of nobles to resolve this, the Anglo-Saxons, using knives concealed in their shoes, betrayed Vortigern by massacring all 460 members of the council, except Vortigern.

To appease them, Vortigern gave them more lands in the south, but the Anglo-Saxons invaded areas across Britain, creating seven major kingdoms: Northumbria, East Anglia, Essex, Sussex, Kent, Wessex (including Berkshire), and Mercia. The West Saxons colonised the area known today as Berkshire and rivalries between kings of Wessex and Mercia saw parts of modern Berkshire change hands several times.

The next threat of invasion to Berkshire came from Danish Vikings, who by 870 controlled the north and the east of England, including Kent. In a pincer movement they moved south and westward towards Wessex. In December 870, the Danes set out to capture the market town, royal residence, and birthplace of King Alfred the Great, known today as Wantage.

Mooring their longboats at Maidenhead, the Danish army, commanded by King Bagsac, arrived at Reading on 28 December and launched a surprise attack on the Saxons stationed there, who abandoned the town in panic. Two days later the Danes' scouting party found the Saxon force at Englefield, 6 miles west of Reading, and unsuccessfully attacked them. The defeated Danes returned to Reading where, four days later, the Saxons, invigorated by

Treachery and betrayal of Vortigern. (NS)

Alfred the Great, Wantage.

their victory and with reinforcements, tried to recapture the town in a clash known today as the First Battle of Reading. Despite fierce fighting, the Danes repelled their attackers, who retreated and at once began rallying men to fight the Danish invaders.

Although the exact location is disputed, most historians agree that the battle took place along the prehistoric Ridgeway path, on land somewhere between Aldworth and Aston Upthorpe. The Saxon army, numbering 1,500, was divided, camping on both Blewburton Hill under the command of King Ethelred and on Kingstanding Hill under the command of his younger brother, Alfred. On 7 January 871, Saxon scouts spotted Bagsac's army of 1,000 men making their way from Reading towards Wantage. Ethelred and Alfred agreed to attack the Danes the following morning in a surprise attack from two different directions. As planned, Alfred led his troops off the hill and marched towards the Danes, not knowing that Ethelred's troops were still deep in prayer and had not begun their advance. Alfred, fearing he would lose the element of surprise by waiting for Ethelred to arrive, launched his attack. His troops, mostly farmers were armed with swords and spears, with only shields for protection, fought uphill against the chainmail-wearing Danes better armed with bows, swords, and battle axes.

Alfred, disadvantaged and outnumbered, was losing the battle when Ethelred's arrival caused the Danes to withdraw. Pursued by the Saxon army they fought a running battle over several miles back to Reading. The fighting lasted all day. Corpses littered the slopes of the Downs for miles, the Saxons had defeated the Danes, killing five of their earls and King Bagsac. For almost 150 years the Saxons and Danes continued to skirmish across the kingdoms of Britain, their marauding campaigns halted only briefly by truces, alliances, and peace treaties.

During the winter of 1006, a Danish army led by King Sweyn Forkbeard left their winter base on the Isle of Wight and raided unopposed through Hampshire, Sussex and Berkshire. The Danes sacked and burned Reading, destroying its abbey before attacking Wallingford and marching back to Southampton Water.

Sixty years later Britain was once more invaded and conquered, this time by a Norman army commanded by William, Duke of Normandy. As with the Romans, the Norman subjugation of Berkshire was a bloodless and somewhat insignificant affair. William arrived at Wallingford, then the major town of Berkshire and residence of Ealdorman Lord Wigod, who invited the invading army into the town to rest before crossing the Thames.

Re-enactors, Wryngwyrm Dark Age Warband.

Stigand, the Archbishop of Canterbury, England's chief administrator and advisor to uncrowned King Edgar Aetheling, met with William en route to London. Stigand abandoned Aetheling, sided with William and surrendered Wallingford and Reading to the duke. He then travelled to Berkhamsted with William and his army, where Edgar and the rest of England's governance surrendered, enabling William to become King of England on Christmas Day 1066.

In the centuries that followed, raiders from France, Spain and the Netherlands repeatedly attacked the coastal counties of Britain. While several invasions were unsuccessful, latterly the French invasion of Fishguard, south-west Wales in 1797, the fear of invasion and further conquests remained a recurring and relentless concern in the minds of the people of Britain.

Berkshire, like other landlocked counties, was spared the horror and humiliation of such bloody and brutal raids. That is until the twentieth century, when in 1939 Germany, once again a military superpower, invaded Poland and began its invasion of Europe.

When the last Allied troops were evacuated from the beaches of Dunkirk in June 1940, Germany's leader, Adolf Hitler, decided to annex Britain, but Prime Minister Winston Churchill rejected French proposals to allow Italy to mediate Britain's surrender. Having failed to secure air supremacy over Britain, Hitler tried to strangle Britain into submission using naval blockades, strategic bombing campaigns, and eventually the V-1 flying bomb and V-2 ballistic missile. While much of Berkshire escaped the carnage of the Luftwaffe's bombing, its transport hubs and areas of military and industrial importance were not so fortunate.

The Berkshire County Air Raid Precautions Officer's records show that from July 1940 to May 1941, 1,595 bombs (not including incendiaries) fell on the county. Between May

1-kg electron incendiary bomb.

500-kg bomb found at Woodley.

1941 and April 1944 attacks on the county were rare, with only 115 bombs dropped. The total number of bombs dropped was 1,710 – 1,595 were high explosive, 105 were oil bombs, and ten were parachute mines. Additionally, on fifty-four occasions 1-kg incendiary bombs were dropped. Although these were not accurately recorded, they are believed to have numbered several thousand.

Hatford, now part of Oxfordshire, was among the first places in Berkshire to suffer fatalities when a lone German Dornier bomber dropped six bombs on the village in September 1940. One landed directly on the off-licence and general stores, killing Mr and Mrs Grainger, their fifteen-year-old daughter Muriel, and their grandsons who were evacuees from London – Jimmy Green (aged six) and Patrick Boyle (aged two); both had sought sanctuary there days earlier.

A week after the tragedy the village held a joint funeral service at St George's Church, conducted by Canon E. Farmer and Revd J. Wilmot. The congregation, which included most of the residents of the village and many from Stanford in the Vale, sang 'Safe in the Arms of Jesus'. Eleven years after the bombing, the off-licence and general stores at the centre of the village remained in ruins.

The village of Woodley and its aerodrome were bombed many times between August 1940 and May 1943, during which several properties were damaged and residents were injured. On 6 October 1940, two women delivering milk and a paperboy had remarkable escapes when a German plane opened fire on them forcing them to take cover in a ditch.

St George's
Church, Hatford.

Similarly, Margaret Wood, a nurse visiting a patient on her bicycle, avoided injury when she was strafed by bullets from a German bomber being chased by a Spitfire. Unnerved, she continued cycling as the bullets exploded all around her. Unfortunately, a number of cows at Holme Park were not so lucky when a wayward bomb exploded in their field.

On 10 February 1943, a lone German Dornier bomber appeared in the skies above Newbury. Having made several flypasts, it dived towards the town and began machine-gunning people and property. Having attacked the school and vicarage at Cold Ash, it then unleashed death and destruction, dropping its payload of four 500-kg and four 50-kg bombs. In all, 265 dwellings were damaged, with St Bartholomew's almshouse, St John's Church, Southampton Terrace, and the Senior Council School being destroyed. During the raid forty-one people were injured – twenty-five seriously. Of the fifteen people killed, two were teachers and three were pupils at the school, which received a direct hit from a 500-kg bomb.

Five minutes earlier the Dornier had dropped four 500-kg bombs on the centre of Reading town, its target the railway station. The attack killed forty-one people and injured 150. The bombs fell in and around Minster Street and Friar Street with the largest concentration of fatalities within the People's Pantry on Duke Street, a restaurant set up to offer cheap meals to supplement rations. Only thirty-seven of the people killed were identified, including two girls aged ten. The horror continued as the German bomber then opened fire with its machine guns, strafing those fleeing for their lives.

Volunteers searching through the rubble afterwards not only discovered human body parts, but also a stone finger belonging to the statue of Queen Victoria in Town Hall Square.

Many wardens and civilians received commendations for bravery during and after the raid. Ms Macrini, an ambulance driver, had been off duty and away from Reading during the attack. Returning home, she learned her father was among the fatalities. The following morning, she reported for duty and worked late into the night conveying bodies and body parts from the scene, despite every effort to persuade her to return home.

During the six months from June to the end of 1944, a dozen of Hitler's vengeance weapons – V-1 flying bombs – fell in Berkshire. Having putted their way over Kent, London, and Surrey, they fell silent before falling from the air, causing death and destruction. March 1945 saw the introduction of Hitler's second vengeance weapon, the V-2 rocket. Faulty gas mains were initially blamed for the explosions. One detonated at Wargrave, causing extensive damage to a cottage. Another seriously injured two people at Cockpole Green, Hurley, the furthest west any V-2 rocket reached in England. In Berkshire, these weapons caused forty-three fatalities, seriously wounding ninety-six people and slightly injuring 181 others.

Since those dark days, developments in technology and science continue to advance warfare beyond the threat of physical tussles between forces fighting for terrain, power, and control. Conventional invasion tactics are being replaced by new tactics that use stealth and cyber technologies to invade and attack from afar defeating the enemy in advance of their physical arrival.

The People's Pantry. (RM)

Town Hall Square. (RM)

V-1 flying bomb.

Above: Aftermath of V-2 attack, Wargrave. (JT)

Left: V-2 (Vergeltungswaffe 2) rocket.

2. Hill Forts to Nuclear Bunkers

Berkshire's earliest military defences are hill forts, fortified earthworks built during the late Bronze and Iron Age periods over 2,000 years ago. As their name suggests, hill forts were located to exploit a natural rise in elevation for defensive advantage.

Tribal chieftains designed their hill forts as strongholds to protect their people and resources during severe weather, attacks from neighbouring or invading tribes and wild animals. They held houses, important buildings, armouries, corrals, workshops and functioned as meeting places, centres for religious celebration, marshalling warriors, and administrating justice. Hill forts, like the Norman castles that followed, were symbolic displays of ostentation, wealth and military might.

Developments in technology saw iron replace bronze, resulting in different styles of hill fort constructions. In Berkshire, the dominant types were the contour, a balustraded hilltop surrounded by artificial ramparts or steep natural slopes on all sides, and the promontory, a structure built on a ridge or spur with steep slopes on two or three sides and artificial ramparts on the other approach. Single, double, or multiple circuits of defensive earthworks surrounded the forts, which, when built in close proximity, offered an effective in-depth system of defence capable of providing proactive or reactive mutual support.

During the 1960s, twenty-one hill forts existed in Berkshire. Following boundary changes between 1974 and 1995, that number is now seven. The new county is ringed by hill forts at Uffington Castle, Segsbury, Rams Hill, Alfred's Castle, and Blewbury on the crest of the Berkshire Downs, with more hill forts on the north bank of the Thames at Bozedown, Taplow, and Medmenham, all originally within Berkshire's boundaries.

Among the county's remaining Iron Age hill forts, Borough and Bussock hill forts were small homesteads, contour forts with single-ditch defences. Borough Hill occupies half an acre and Bussock Camp 10 acres, with additional double-ditch defences at its north, south, and east sides. A survey of the north and western defences during the late 1800s records them being between 12 and 20 feet in height. Although gravel quarrying has since denuded these, the surviving banks and ditches on the southern side are 33 feet across.

Segsbury Camp is a large hill fort cut in two by a road on a chalk plateau running east to west, north of the Ridgeway track, with commanding views of the plains and village of Letcombe Regis below. A univallate hill fort, it includes a rampart bank standing 10 feet above the interior, beyond which lies an external ditch 66 feet wide and 22 feet deep.

Grimsbury Castle remains a well-preserved contour hill fort located south of Hermitage. Constructed on a promontory, unusually it originally had three entrances and enclosed 8 acres of plateau, with substantial outworks stretching 240 feet from its western defences. The remains of Grimsbury's ramparts are visible and in places exceed 10 feet in height. Today woodland covers the fort, and a road allows visitors to drive through the defences. By contrast, following centuries of farming Perborough Castle once a 14-acre

Segsbury Hill Fort.

site has been all but ploughed out, with only the northernmost part of the site remaining, showing a simple gap and causeway entrance.

Berkshires largest hill fort is the kite-shaped Walbury Camp, built during the Iron Age in an area of around 82 acres. The banks do not appear high, although when viewed from below the scarp outside the top of the rampart on the north side rises to 16 feet above the ditch bottom. Access to the fort was via gates, long gone, in the north-west and south-east ramparts. At the north-west entrance a hollow path runs through two outworks across the neck of the hill with additional banks connected to its terminals, producing a barbican-like structure.

Today, Membury Camp, north-west of Hungerford, straddles the borders of Wiltshire and Berkshire. Encompassing 34 acres, its defences comprised a ditch sandwiched between two impressive banks. A flanking diagonal outwork defended the original entrance on the north-east side, but in 1942 construction workers destroyed it to make way for a wartime airfield, RAF Membury, which in turn was replaced by Membury Airfield Industrial Estate.

With its curious oak leaf shape, Caesar's Camp at Bracknell is one of the most distinctive Iron Age hill forts in Britain. The fort takes its name from the erroneous belief by early historians that it was a Roman camp, created by Julius Caesar during his campaign of CE 55–54. Archaeological evidence shows the site to be a large Iron Age contour hill fort with defensive banks and ditches. Following the Roman invasion of CE 84, the Romans occupied the fort while they established local rule. Archaeologists have found Roman and Romano-British coins, including a sliver coin of the pre-Roman King of Britain, Cunobelin. In places the main rampart is a massive bank 12 feet high by 45 feet wide, enclosing over 25 acres. Along its eastern side and other points along the perimeter

Walbury Hill Fort.

runs another ditch and bank. The entrances are at its southern and northern ends. The southern entrance survives as a buried feature, while excavations revealed the remains of a sub-square redoubt 120 feet across and believed to be part of a larger defence line created during military exercises in 1792.

Despite the ravages of time, weather and war, the remains of Berkshires hill forts are impressive and in places the banks remain formidable obstacles. One can only marvel at the magnitude of these structures when imagining their former glory, topped with tall, imposing palisades of wood, and earth ramparts reinforced with stone.

Defending the fort was a tribal responsibility, with men and women fighting on the palisades. Archaeological excavations show that Iron Age warriors used long swords as slashing weapons, javelins, and leather shields overlaid with bronze for protection. Their weapon of choice was the slingshot – easy and inexpensive to make, with a range of 600 to 1,000 feet. Shooting from a hill fort's ramparts or palisades a skilled slinger could accurately hit their target up to 90 feet. A relentless and deadly form of warfare, excavations at larger hill fort sites repeatedly show stockpiles of tens of thousands of stones at strategic points around the fort's defences.

On returning power and lands to King Verica c. CE 42, the Romans occupied and refortified major hill forts as military bases, governing the local populace from those bases while completing the process of Romanisation. Part of Verica's kingdom was the Iron Age capital of the Atrebates, near modern-day Silchester (now in Hampshire). The Romans took control of the town, where they administrated the region, collected taxes, and executed justice.

They renamed the town Calleva Atrebatum and fortified it with large walls. The defences offered sufficient protection from local uprisings or pillaging raids from invaders abroad and also allowed the local administration to monitor traffic. Evidence of Atrebatum's prosperity is the dual carriageway and contra-flow system running between

Fortified walls of Calleva Atrebatum.

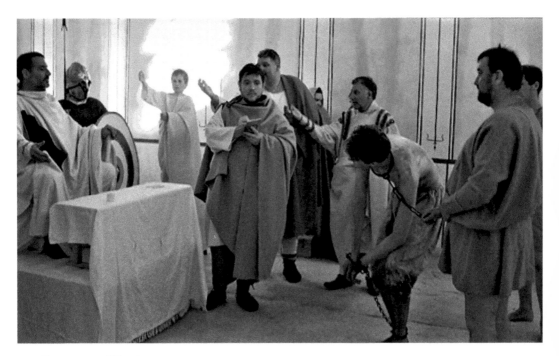

Re-enactors of Comitatus.

the eastern and western gates (leading to London and Exeter respectively) Substantial remains of the wall exist, together with wall projections along the inner face of the town wall where fighting platforms once existed, and at the south gate there are the bases of guard chambers.

The Romans constructed a system of roads across the Thames Valley that connected and networked their new towns, villas, and farmsteads. They kept a small military presence within each town and fortified outposts at strategic sites such as river and road crossings. Some, in time, became large, fortified villas like Littlecote. Some soldiers were also garrisoned at posting stations (rectangular fortified sites) found at regular intervals along the Roman roads where official messengers could change horses, and marching troops and travellers could rest in safety from thieves and raiders.

Atrebatum grew into a major trading centre, where the Atrebates exchanged manufactured goods for metals, grain, slaves, and other commodities with traders from across the south of Britain. The remains of the town walls are some of the best-preserved examples of Roman town defences in England.

The Saxon king Alfred the Great created the county's next defensive structures as part of his system to defend the kingdom of Wessex (Berkshire, Hampshire, Wiltshire, Dorset, Somerset) against Viking attacks. Alfred built thirty-three burhs (fortified towns) across Wessex, sited on hilltops, river crossings and overlooking harbours.

Alfred repaired and reinforced, old hill forts and Roman towns, while enclosing other towns with massive earthen walls, wide ditches, fortified wooden revetments, and

Remains of Wallingford burgh.

tall palisades. Alfred sited the burhs 20 miles apart so that no person was more than a day's travel from protection. Likewise, attackers could be engaged anywhere across the kingdom within a day. Alfred organised his army to serve on a rota basis, with noblemen and peasants taking turns tending farms and serving in the army. A system of roads connected the burhs, enabling the army to assemble and move quickly to confront any threat posed by the invading Vikings.

In Berkshire, Alfred built large burhs at Wallingford and on Sashes Island, Cookham. A great wall, 9,900 feet in length, encircled Wallingford. It had a high earthen bank and steep ditches that enclosed 100 acres, providing protection for 2,400 people.

When they arrived in 1066, the Normans, like the Romans, occupied hill forts and built temporary motte-and-bailey (a mound with a tower on top and a wooden wall enclosing a living area) castles in strategic areas. Once the Normans gained control of the Saxon tribes, they built more substantial and imposing stone castles, often on the site of temporary castles. From there they imposed their rule upon the Saxon people.

Berkshire, being landlocked, had little need for defensive castles and, as England recognised Norman rule, its main defence against invasion came from the surrounding counties. In the decade after the Conquest, William I established a defensive ring of motte-and-bailey castles around London. Like Alfred's burhs, each was a day's march from the city and the nearest castle. One of these castles was Windsor, a key route into London and strategically important because of its proximity to the River Thames. Rebuilt in stone, it was constantly upgraded, developed, and expanded while retaining its original motte-and-bailey shape. Today the castle is a royal residence and a major tourist attraction.

Artist impression of a motte-and-bailey castle.

Above: Windsor Castle.

Right: Remains of Donnington Castle.

At Donnington in 1386, Sir Richard Abberbury the Elder, a royal chamberlain, built the mighty Donnington Castle. Destroyed during the English Civil War (1642–51), only the striking twin-towered gatehouse and foundations remain. Likewise, at Wallingford only the ruins are viewable of the Norman fortified bridge and great castle.

While successive monarchs reinforced the defences of coastal counties to counter weapon advancements and threats of invasion, inland nobility and members of the aristocracy financed and built personal defences. Often referred to as castles, these were fortified houses, moated properties, or castellated mansions. All of which have disappeared with no trace or exist as basic earthworks such as the fortified manor houses of Buckland, Shellingford, Cumnor, Southcote, and Chamberhouse and the timber castles at Faringdon, Newbury, and Reading.

Despite centuries of threats, Berkshire did little to fortify the county. It wasn't until 1940, when Britain was at war with Germany and invasion became a real possibility, that Berkshire's landscape changed to accommodate a defensive system of fortifications known as the General Headquarters Line (GHQ Line).

Britain had heavily fortified its coastline in 1939, but it wasn't until 1940, when France fell and the Allies were evacuated from Dunkirk, that it began preparing for a German invasion. Intended to protect London and the industrial heart of Britain, the GHQ Line or Stop Line as it became known was a static system of over fifty defensive lines. Its purpose was to compartmentalise the country and delay the Germans long enough to enable mobile forces to counterattack. These lines would be the nation's last chance of defence.

FW3/28 anti-tank pillbox, Hungerford Common.

FW3/22 shell-proof pillbox, Dunmill Lock.

A stop line entered Berkshire at Swallowfield, continued to Reading following the A33 corridor, where it followed the Kennet and Avon Canal as far as the western county boundary. The line comprised 'nodal points', locations along roads, railways or waterways that connected two villages or towns fitted with anti-tank obstacles, various pillboxes, and gun emplacements.

Following the war landowners were paid to demolish these defences, but remnants of the line and nodal points still exist. Among those listed as monuments are the anti-tank and shellproof field defences at Hungerford Common, anti-tank girder at Enborne, and anti-tank blocks at Kintbury. The county's sole surviving Vickers machine machine-gun emplacement is close to Junction 11, M4, and at Burghfield a two-storey brick-built building and stable block was fortified to provide a shellproof infantry strongpoint. Nationally, 6,000 pillboxes survive; in Berkshire 150 are designated monuments. Squat concrete forts, pillboxes pay a silent tribute to the courage and tenacity of the British people during the dark days of the Second World War.

More recently Berkshire played an important strategic role in the nation's defence against nuclear attack during the forty-year Cold War with the USSR. In response to the escalating tension between the USSR and newly formed North Atlantic Treaty Organization (NATO), the Civil Defence (Public Protection) Regulations of 1949 set up a Civil Defence Corps (CDC).

The CDC was a civilian organisation, created in 1949 to mobilise and take local control of affected areas in the aftermath of a nuclear attack. If a nuclear strike happened, the Royal Observer Corps (ROC) were tasked with staffing bunkers, or 'monitoring posts', from which they would observe radiation levels in their area.

Above: Fortified building, Burfield.

Left: Royal Observer Corps monitoring post.

Built to a standard design 15 feet below ground, bunkers were accessed via a surface hatch and ladder leading to a monitoring room with bunk beds, a toilet, communications, and monitoring equipment. Over 1,500 underground bunkers were built across the country, with each accommodating a team of three men. Grouped in clusters of three to four posts connected via VHF radio and telephone to their group's HQ, sector HQ and regional HQ.

Now demolished, ROC bunkers were located at Great Shefford, East Ilsley, Crowthorne, Cold Ash, Arborfield and Newbury. At Windsor, Bradfield, Ascot, Shurlock and Streatly bunkers survive in varying conditions.

Berkshire housed key governmental, political, military and police personnel in several Cold War emergency centres and local authority bunkers. Like the ROC posts, most no longer exist. Region 6 (Berkshire, Buckinghamshire, Dorset, Hampshire, Oxfordshire, and the Isle of Wight) War Room remains on the Whiteknights Park campus of the University of Reading. Built during the 1950s, the bunker housed one of eleven regional commissioners and their staff. Following an attack on the country by conventional or atomic bombs, they would be responsible for co-ordinating the strategic civil defence response across the region. If contact with central government failed, the commissioner would assume the full power of the central government in their region.

Region Six War Room, Reading University campus. (CC)

Protected by vast concrete walls and filtration towers, the bunker's upper level is above ground and lower-level underneath. When the Regional War Rooms were replaced by regional seats of government, the Region 6 War Room transferred to a secret bunker at the former Second World War underground aircraft components factory in the chalk mines at Warren Row, Maidenhead. Now used by MJF Data Management Ltd, the bunker was once used to store wine.

Another nuclear bunker now being used for storage was built during 1959 at Eton College beneath one of the boys' houses. Constructed as an integral part of the building it provided accommodation for forty-eight people including the governing body of Eton College known as 'the provost and fellows'. these were a provost (appointed by the Crown), a vice-provost, and ten fellows.

A Victorian mansion stands at East Hampstead Park on the edge of Wokingham. During the 1960s the Secretary of State authorised its cellar to be converted to an emergency nuclear bunker to function as the Bracknell and East Berkshire (Sub) County Control Nuclear Bunker.

Berkshire's most famous cold war connection was its military air base at Greenham Common Airfield, part of the notorious 'nuclear valley', trio of Burghfield, Aldermaston and Greenham.

From 1951 to 1992, Greenham Common was an American airbase. The United States Air Force (USAF) extended the runway to 12,000 feet in 1980, making it the longest in

Victorian mansion, Easthampstead.

Europe. The first nuclear missiles arrived on 14 November 1983 and at its height it housed ninety-six ground-launched nuclear Cruise missiles in six silos at the base. The 1987 treaty between the USA and the USSR ordered Greenham's Cruise missiles removed for destruction. The USAF handed the airbase back to the RAF in 1992, and in April 2000 the people of Newbury reclaimed it. The Cold War control tower is now a visitor centre with a permanent exhibition about the era.

During the late 1940s the former wartime airfield, Aldermaston, became the permanent home of The Atomic Weapons Research Establishment (AWRE) and Britain's nuclear weapons programme. In 1987 the AWRE became the Atomic Weapons Establishment, placing its two nuclear Ordnance Factories Burghfield and Cardiff under Aldermaston's control. The site has been the scene of frequent protest by peace activists, starting with the Campaign for Nuclear Disarmament march from London to Aldermaston in 1958.

Aldermaston was a weapons research and design centre, while Burghfield, a former munitions factory, performed production and assembly functions. Among the nuclear weapons developed by scientists at Aldermaston were the 'Blue Danube' Mk 1 atom bomb; 'Yellow Sun', Britain's first operational high-yield strategic nuclear weapon; and the Polaris system.

Greenham Common Control Tower.

Protestors at Greenham Common.

Their association with the Cruise missile programme resulted in 70,000 protestors joining women at Greenham Common in 1983 to form a human chain that connected Greenham to Aldermaston and Burghfield, stretching over 14 miles. Today both sites play a key role in keeping the nation safe through the manufacture, maintenance, and development of warheads for Britain's ultimate nuclear deterrent Trident.

3. Revolution and Rebellion

Following the death of Henry I in 1135, a fierce battle for the throne of England began between Henry's nephew, Stephen of Blois, and his daughter and only legitimate heir, Empress Matilda. Stephen claimed the throne, saying his uncle had named him as his successor on his deathbed. Having sworn loyalty to Matilda during Henry's lifetime, upon his death England's powerful barons switched fidelity to Stephen. Matilda, supported by her half-brother Robert Earl of Gloucester, rejected the claim and a civil war now known as the Anarchy (1135–53) ensued.

During this period several battles took place, with both sides besieging the other's strongholds. Robert's power base was Gloucestershire, but included a great deal of southern Wales, south-west England, and some of Berkshire. At Wallingford, then in Berkshire, the castle, held by Brian Fitz-Count, became a major power base for forces loyal to Matilda when he declared his support for her.

In 1139, Stephen's army besieged Wallingford Castle and its garrison, but the walls proved impregnable, so he set about building two counter-castles in Wallingford to prevent any attempt by Matilda's supporters to influence and control territory further east. A year later the Earl of Gloucester sent Miles Fitz-Walter of Gloucester, 1st Earl of Hereford, to support

Remains of Wallingford Castle.

the beleaguered Fitz-Count. With complete surprise he attacked the siege force, destroying one of the two counter-castles and ousted Stephen's forces from the other. Stephen returned to lay siege to the castle in 1445 and 1152, but the castle's formidable defences proved too strong for them to take the castle. The castle remained an imposing defence until its destruction by Parliamentary forces in June 1646 following a long siege.

Undeterred, Stephen moved his army to Newbury in late 1152 where he besieged the castle under the control of John Marshal, a former knight of Stephen's. Marshal, nearing defeat, bought himself some time by signing a truce with Stephen and agreeing to plead with Matilda to allow him to surrender. Marshal had no intentions of surrendering the castle and used the break in hostilities to fill the keep to capacity with men and supplies, before telling Stephen he would not surrender.

Newbury remained under siege for two months until Stephen and Matilda signed the Treaty of Wallingford in November 1153. Having acknowledged Stephen as king, he agreed Matilda's son Henry of Anjou would become his heir. A year later, Stephen died and Henry became King Henry II. Following Henry II's death in 1189, Richard I, succeeded him as king. Richard spent much of his early reign away from England fighting in the Third Crusade. During 1192, Richard's younger brother, Prince John, led a rebellion to usurp Richard and plotted to have him kidnapped and imprisoned.

In 1193, to increase his power John seized and garrisoned Windsor Castle. Richard responded by sending the Archbishop of Rouen, Walter de Coutances, back to England with a force of loyal knights commanded by his top military advisor, Baron William Marshal, who laid siege to John and his forces at Windsor.

Treaty of Wallingford, 1153.

Following a protracted siege William Marshal took the castle, although Prince John and his men escaped. John lost power, revenue, and lands in France following a series of disastrous military campaigns against Philip II. The castle was next besieged during the revolt by England's barons in 1214. John, now king, used the castle as his base to avoid a civil war before signing the Magna Carta on 15 June 1215. When John refused to accept or abide by its terms and had the pope declare it invalid, civil war became inevitable.

Baronial and French troops once more besieged Windsor in 1216 under the command of the Count of Nevers, son of Philip II. Despite trebuchets, ballistae, battering rams and siege towers severely damaging the castle, sixty knights led by Constable Engelard de Cigogné successfully defended it for six months.

Like King John, Henry III's autocratic rule of excessive taxation, and promotion of foreign favourites provoked England's barons. In 1263, discontent plunged the country into another civil war. The barons, spurred on by Henry's brother-in-law Simon de Montfort, Earl of Leicester, sought to implement the charter 'the Provisions of Oxford' requiring Henry III to surrender his powers concerning taxation and inheritance to a council headed by de Montfort and overseen by a Great Council (Parliament). Henry III asked Louis IX of France to act as arbitrator and, in January 1264, in 'The Mise of Amiens', he annulled the Provisions of Oxford – a decision that led to the Second Barons War (1264–67) with the rebel faction headed by de Montfort.

Each side began taking key castles and several battles ensued. In Berkshire, de Montfort had hoped to secure Windsor before his rebellion became known, but Prince Edward got there first. De Montfort and other barons compelled Henry to demand that Edward surrendered the castle.

When de Montfort arrived at Windsor with a large army and orders from Henry to surrender, Prince Edward refused. A short siege followed before, on 26 July 1263, the prince negotiated a truce agreeing terms of surrender that allowed him and his force of Flemish soldiers to leave the castle, with their horses and arms, and return to France.

Windsor Castle witnessed royal treachery and revolt during the reign of Henry IV in 1399, when rebels loyal to the deposed Richard II plotted an insurrection, which would see the imprisoned monarch returned to his throne. Led by John Montagu, 3rd Earl of Salisbury, John Holland, 1st Earl of Huntingdon, and Thomas Holland, 3rd Earl of Kent, they planned to assassinate Henry and his sons during the winter festival of Epiphany Eve.

On learning of the threat, Henry moved the festival from Oxford to Berkshire and the safety of the Windsor Castle. There, a minor conspirator, the Earl of Rutland, reconsidered and sent Henry a warning that assassins disguised as mummers (groups of masked persons who performed plays) would try to kill him. Henry immediately left for London and later that evening, on 4 January 1400, a rebellious army of 400 armed horsemen led by the earls and dressed as performers entered Windsor Castle unchallenged. The earls searched fruitlessly for the king and his sons only to learn they had fled for London hours earlier having discovered the plan.

The earls fled. Montague headed westwards in open rebellion, raising support for the insurrection and encouraging royalists to rise up and fight for Richard. To give Montague time to raise more men, Thomas Holland blocked Henry's army first at Colnbrook and then at Maidenhead by blockading the bridge. Montague rode to Reading looking for support before travelling to Wallingford and Abingdon. Throughout the Vale of the White Horse, Salisbury incited people to fight Henry. Desperate, Montague produced a priest at Faringdon who looked like Richard, claiming that it was him.

The battle for Maidenhead Bridge lasted three days before Holland's forces were overcome. The earl, having secured provisions for his men, fled to find Montague. The royal forces crossed the bridge in close pursuit of the rebels. Thomas Holland caught up with Montague at Cirencester, where citizens loyal to Henry arrested the earls and several high-ranking associates. A rescue attempt was botched and an angry mob of townspeople executed the earls and their allies.

John Holland and other rebel earls were executed without trial, their heads placed on poles across London Bridge for all to see. Henry oversaw the execution of twenty-nine rebel knights and squires in the Green Ditch outside the town walls of Oxford. The rest went to London for trial. The rebellion convinced Henry that, although imprisoned, Richard was a serious threat. By February Richard had mysteriously died at Pontefract Castle.

Eighty-three years later the county featured in another armed insurrection. The first threat to the Yorkist usurper Richard III's kingship came just four months after his coronation in October 1483, when his closest and most powerful ally, Henry Stafford, Duke of Buckingham, plotted to replace him with Henry Tudor, Earl of Richmond.

While the Duke of Buckingham raised forces in Wales, five risings across the south and west of England were being prepared. On St Luke's Day, 18 October 1483, Sir William Berkley, Sir John Harcourt, Sir William Norreys of Yattendon and Thomas de la Mare of Aldermaston took up arms, raising the standard of revolt at Newbury. Answering Buckingham's call to arms they rallied their men, proclaiming Henry Tudor as King of England. Buckingham mobilised the rising and left Wales to join the army, but a storm flooded the River Severn, preventing him from joining his confederates.

The dukes were betrayed, taken to Salisbury and beheaded. Richard offered large sums of money for the other leaders and many insurgents sought sanctuary in religious places, like Sir Thomas de la Mare at Sion Abbey. Others, like Sir William Norreys, escaped to Brittany or left for Europe.

During the English Civil War of 1642–51 Newbury once more became the scene of rebellion when it hosted two battles. At 7 a.m. on 20 September 1643 a Parliamentarian army commanded by Robert Devereux, 3rd Earl of Essex, was met en route to London by the Royalist army under the command of Charles I and Prince Rupert of the Rhine.

Charles had 14,000 men, 6,000 of which were horse and dragoons, plus twenty cannons. Essex's forces totalled 15,000 men, 4,000 horse and dragoons with an unknown number of cannons.

The two sides clashed south-west of Newbury, where deep lanes and fields banked by hedgerows, covered much of the terrain. These features nullified Charles's cavalry advantage but allowed Essex to exploit infantry superiority. The Royalists deployed first, but Essex made better use of the ground as the battle unfolded across Wash Common, over Round Hill and among the surrounding land for twelve hours. Then, with supplies of black powder and musket shot running low, the Royalists withdrew.

Above left: Henry Stafford, 2nd Duke of Buckingham.

Above right: Robert Devereux, 3rd Earl of Essex.

Re-enactment of the Battle of Newbury. (© Sealed Knot)

About 3,500 men died that day, the greater proportion among the Royalists who had lost their brigade commander, the Earl of Caernarvon, Robert Dormer, Lord Sunderland, Henry Spencer, 1st Earl of Sunderland, and the King's Secretary of State, Lord Falkland, Lucius Cary, 2nd Viscount, who, depressed by the fratricidal conflict, deliberately charged himself and his men into the heart of the action. In all, eleven Royalist and six Parliamentary colonels died. This gave neither side a decisive advantage. Horrified by the bloodshed, Charles I refused to renew the struggle the next day and headed to Oxford, enabling Devereux to continue his march to London.

A year later, Newbury saw a second battle. It began at 3 p.m. on 25 October after Royalist forces, 4,000 cavalry and 5,500 infantry commanded by Charles I gathered north of Newbury at Speenhamland between the rivers Kennet and Lambourne. The Parliamentarian forces of the Earl of Essex, Sir William Waller and the Earl of Manchester, consisting of 7,300 cavalry and 9,300 infantry, came together on Bucklebury Heath to the east of Newbury and advanced along the Bath Road before defeating Royalist troops to take Clay Hill and overlook the Royalists.

The next day the Parliamentarians split into two forces and attacked the Royalists from the east and the west. After marching north overnight the western force attacked the Royalists around Speen, driving them out of their defensive positions. The eastern force attacked the Royalists, in defensive positions around Shaw House, an Elizabethan mansion that served as Charles I's headquarters. Despite early success, the Parliamentarians were

Second Battle of Newbury. (PM)

Donnington Grove, site of the Second Battle of Newbury.

forced back from Shaw House. Losses for the day stood at 500–700 killed on both sides. Once again there had been no decisive victory. Overnight, the Royalists beat a hasty retreat to Oxford, leaving their cannon at Donnington Castle. Parliamentarian forces lay siege to the castle. Under the remarkable leadership of Lieutenant-Colonel John Boys, Donnington forces repeatedly repelled Parliamentary forces. When the defenders eventually surrendered, they marched out with drums beating and their colours flying – a recognition of their outstanding gallantry. Boys was later knighted by Charles I for his defence of Donnington Castle.

The Civil War came to Reading with a bloody vengeance. On 14 April 1642, Robert Devereux, captain general and chief commander of the Parliamentarian army, and his army of 16,000 infantry, 3,000 cavalry and a train of artillery, demanded the surrender of Sir Arthur Aston and his garrison of 2,000 troops. Aston refused. In response, Parliamentarian troops seized Caversham Bridge to prevent Royalist reinforcements arriving from Oxford. Devereux set up gun batteries and established a headquarters in an old, moated manor house. This did not prevent Aston's reinforcements from getting through. 600 musketeers and a supply of ammunition arriving from Sonning by boat.

The Parliamentarian guns began firing upon the town in the morning of Sunday 16 April, and Aston's cannon returned fire using St Giles' Church tower as a gun platform. Consequently, it was attacked by artillery and the upper part of the tower, including its spire, was destroyed, although it was restored following the war.

Shaw House, Newbury.

Charles I, fearing the loss of Reading, recalled Prince Rupert from his siege of Lichfield in the Midlands. During a bombardment on 19 April, a piece of broken chimney pot struck Ashton on the head, leaving him speechless. His deputy, Colonel Richard Fielding, took command.

On 25 April, Fielding called a truce and negotiated a conditional surrender with Devereux. Later that day Rupert and the Royalist force arrived. Unaware of the truce, Charles and Rupert, supported by their guns, led a charge against the Parliamentary guard holding Caversham Bridge. The narrowness of the bridge meant they had no space to move and were an easy target. Fielding refused to break the truce and allow troops from the town to help, and the Royalists failed to cross the bridge. A sudden storm of hail and rain completed their discomfort and they withdrew, pursued by the victorious Parliamentarians, leaving many dead and wounded behind. The king, being made aware of the surrender, capitulated, and upon agreeing terms surrendered on 27 April. The Royalist garrison marched to Oxford, leaving Devereux's soldiers holding Reading where for two days they ransacked the town.

While there were many skirmishes between Royalist and Parliamentarian forces across Berkshire, one notable battle was the heroic defence of Farringdon in May 1644. It resulted in the church losing its steeple, the manor house being demolished and over 300 families becoming homeless. In 1645, Farringdon's garrison contained 300 soldiers under the control of the Royalist's commander, Colonel Lisle. When Oliver Cromwell's cavalry overran the town supported by 600 infantry, they unsuccessfully assaulted the Royalist garrison entrenched at Farringdon House. Cromwell launched his attack at 3 a.m. from multiple directions using ladders to scale the walls. The first ten ladder men were captured, fourteen more were killed and several were wounded, causing Cromwell to abandon the attack.

Faringdon became one of the last bastions of Royalist resistance. In April 1646, Parliamentary forces, commanded by Sir Robert Pye, returned. Royalist sharpshooters and posemen (women dressed as soldiers armed with long-barrelled muskets), impeded their progress by firing from the tower of All Saints' Church. Muster roles show that 48 per cent of the Royalist combat strength were men and 52 per cent were women, of which 42 per cent were posemen. Such was the threat posed by the sharpshooters that Pye placed a gun battery on Folly Hill and ordered a bombardment of the church, which killed several sharpshooters.

Heavy cannon fire damaged the steeple, so it was at risk of falling on the Royalist lines. As a result, the Royalists toppled the steeple to fall away from their lines. The bombardment caused substantial damage and many townhouses caught fire. Despite repeated attacks on Farringdon House, the Parliamentarians could not dislodge the defenders so lay siege to it. Two months later, on 24 June, with the house in ruins, Charles I ordered its surrender. The following day he surrendered the Royalist headquarters at Oxford, ending the Civil War.

Civil War Re-enactors, Newbury. (© Sealed Knot).

Cannonball, All Saints' Church, Faringdon.

It wasn't long before Berkshire was once more featured in an attempt to depose a monarch. James II became King of England, Scotland, and Ireland in 1685. His zealous promotion of Catholicism and pursuit of complete religious toleration and civic equality for Catholics and Protestant dissenters made him unpopular, as did his appointment of Catholics to top military, political, and academic positions, which caused the king to prorogue Parliament and rule alone.

Several distinguished Englishmen, including one bishop and prominent politicians from both parties, wrote to William Prince of Orange, James II's nephew and husband to his daughter Mary, inviting him to redress the nation's grievances and claim the throne. William landed at Brixham, Devon, on 5 November 1688 with 14,000 Dutch, French, Brandenburg, Swedish and Finnish soldiers, and marched on London. On 6 December, William and an army swelled with English deserters reached Hungerford. At the Bear Inn he met with representatives of James II to negotiate the terms of his removal as king.

At the same time James II garrisoned 600 Catholic troops, Irish dragoons, and Scottish cavalry at Reading. Their arrival terrified the people, who believed the Irish soldiers were planning to massacre them and plunder the town. They were so fearful that many ran away before the Irish commander placed guards on the exits to the town.

William received a smuggled message from the inhabitants begging for deliverance from the Irishmen and dispatched a Dutch force of 150 infantry and 500 dragoons (mounted infantry) to Reading. Warned of their arrival and believing they would enter the town on the western road, the Irish commander formed calvary in the yard of the Bear Inn, Castle Street. Along the walls of Saint Mary's churchyard, he placed musketeers and mustered infantry in Broad Street. The defender's main forces gathered in the marketplace. The Dutch, also forewarned, approached from Oxford Road (then Pangbourne Lane) and, hidden by high hedges, they entered the town unnoticed.

In the ensuing confusion troops in Broad Street and Castle Street went into the marketplace. Their stampede spread panic, causing the total force to flee. The Irish lost their colours, with fifty men killed and forty captured. Only five Dutch soldiers died; several are buried in St Giles churchyard. This was the only military encounter in an otherwise bloodless coup that saw James II flee, and William and Mary become King and Queen of England, Ireland, and Scotland.

St Giles' Church, Reading.

4. Last Stands and Heroes

Before the English Civil War (1642–51) England had no permanent army. In times of war the king called upon the services of local militias and reserve volunteers. When war broke out between the Royalists and Parliamentarians, they filled their armies with men of the militia and other volunteers, usually unwilling tenants and servants forced to join regiments raised by their landowners.

In 1660, Charles II regained the throne. Believing the Crown needed the protection of an army, he created an army of seven regiments of foot and four mounted regiments. These were part of the royal household and the king's bodyguards.

The country's main force would be the militia. Acts of Parliament made a county's lord lieutenant responsible for organising their county's militia. Although the king commanded all forces, he did not provide central funding, and the cost of men and equipment fell on property owners. In times of national emergency, the militia policed the public, kept the peace, and defended the nation.

Berkshire's militia was first activated in early 1666, during the Second Anglo-Dutch War (1665–67) when Parliament sent 300 men to help defend the Isle of Wight. Following the Treaty of Breda on 31 July 1667, they returned to Berkshire. In the years that followed the militia proved slow to mobilise, thus the regular army was used to crush the Monmouth Rebellion in 1685 and the king expanded his army by sixteen new regiments. After that

Victorian cap badge, 66th Berkshire Regiment.

'General Musters' of the militia were infrequent and, as the size of the regular army increased, the role of the militia in national defence diminished. Until, in 1756, war with France forced another reorganisation of Britain's forces and further increases in regular regiments.

It was then that Parliament ordered several existing regiments to raise second battalions. These battalions would become regiments in their own right, such as the 19th Regiment of Foot (the Green Howards), whose 2nd Battalion became the 66th Regiment of Foot in 1758. The regiment was given a county designation as the 66th (Berkshire) Regiment of Foot in 1782.

Renewed invasion fears saw militias reformed, and on 25 July 1757, 560 men commanded by the Duke of St Albans founded the Berkshire Militia. Between 1756 and 1815 war became commonplace, resulting in compulsory militia recruitment for a three-year term of service. Militias were either 'embodied' or 'disembodied'. Embodied militias resided in a camp or barracks and restricted to service in the United Kingdom but treated on par with regular infantry. The only requirement of disembodied militias was to attend an annual camp.

In 1794, yeomanry (auxiliary regiments) were formed as light cavalry to counter the threat of invasion during the French Revolutionary Wars (1792–1802). The Berkshire Yeomanry first saw active service during the Second Boer War (1899–1902). Later, during the First World War, in April 1915, the regiment sailed for Cairo, Egypt. After several months they moved as infantry to Gallipoli, where in August they met their first enemy action fighting the Turkish. After three months in the trenches, the regiment, less 100 men caring for the horses, withdrew, their strength reduced by casualties and sickness from

Officer, Royal Berkshire Yeomanry Cavalry, 1896.

Boer War, 2nd Royal Berkshire Regiment. (NAM)

Mounted
trooper, 1914.
(HVM)

450 to fifty men. During the Second World War, Berkshire Yeomanry performed another role as field artillery. Today it exists as 94 Signal Squadron, part of 39 Signal Regiment.

In 1803, the 1st Battalion 66th (Berkshire) Regiment of Foot sailed to Ceylon, then on to Calcutta and Nepal to support British operations against the Gurkhas before returning to India in 1816. The 2nd Battalion sailed for the Iberian Peninsula in 1809. During its first action crossing the River Douro at Oporto, Portugal, the battalion suffered the highest casualties of any unit involved – thirty-eight offices and soldiers killed or wounded.

They also fought at Talavera, Spain, where they lost fifteen officers and eighty-three other ranks during the Battle of Busaco in 1810. A year later, French lancers reduced the battalion from 600 to fifty-two men at the Battle of Albuera Spain, before relief arrived.

The regiment's losses were so great they should have returned home, but instead merged with the 31st (Huntingdonshire) Regiment of Foot to form the 1st Provisional Battalion, remaining in service until the end of the war. They fought with distinction at Vitoria, Spain, and in battles in France at Nievelle, Nive, and Orthes, claiming nine regimental battle honours. During July 1817, the 2nd Battalion left India, joining the 1st Battalion in Saint Helena guarding the deposed Emperor Napoleon and were among the soldiers who carried Bonaparte's body to his grave in 1821.

In the following decades, the 66th served in Canada, Barbados, India, and Afghanistan and it was in Afghanistan during the Second Anglo-Afghan War, at Maiwand, near Kandahar on 27 July 1880, six companies of the 66th took their place in history. After enduring hours of fierce fighting against overwhelming numbers of Ghazi (Muslim warriors).

Peninsular War, Battle of Albuera. (TS)

British forces and most of the 66th were routed. 120 made a stand at the Mundabad Ravine, along the south side of the battlefield, but were forced back with heavy losses. His men falling, commanding officer Lieutenant Colonel James Galbraith withdrew to a walled garden where they made a second stand until only two officers and nine men remained. In one final heroic act the eleven men charged out from the garden formed back-to-back and fired at their enemy. Such was their heroism that although surrounded by thousands of Ghazi, not one dared approach, instead they fired at them from a distance until the last man fell. Only then did they seize the regimental colours. Of the nineteen officers and 427 ranks that started the battle, ten officers and 275 men died, and two officers and thirty-one men suffered injuries.

In 1873, Edward Cardwell, Minister of War under Gladstone, introduced his plan for the reorganisation of the infantry of the line. This was a gradual process culminating in the complete amalgamation of many regiments in 1881, when the Secretary of State for War, Hugh Childers, reorganised the infantry regiments. As a result, the 66th (Berkshire) Regiment of Foot merged with the Princess Charlotte of Wales Hertfordshire Regiment, formerly the 49th Hertfordshire Regiment of Foot to become the 1st and 2nd battalions of the Princess Charlotte of Wales's (Berkshire) Regiment.

It was then that the regiment received its nickname, the 'Biscuit Boys', as it was garrisoned permanently at Reading, a town synonymous with the biscuit manufactures Huntley and Palmers. The largest biscuit manufacturer in the world during the

The Last Stand, Battle of Maiwand. (HP)

nineteenth and most of the twentieth century, they supplied biscuits to the British Army for many years.

During the Mahdist War (1881–99), Queen Victoria granted the regiment the title of 'Royal' following the Battle of Tofrek, on the coast of the Sudan, in 1885. She also changed the colour of their uniform facings from white to royal blue.

General McNeill and British forces sent to quash a revolt led by local chieftain Osman Digna, included the 1st Battalion of the Princess Charlotte of Wales's (Berkshire) Regiment. With them in the Suakin area of the Sudan were a battalion of Royal Marines, three Indian regiments, and a squadron of cavalry.

On 26 March, the force was constructing field camp defences among the scrub and thorn bushes when thousands of armed Arabs launched a surprise attack. Although some Arabs got through, the Berkshires armed before the main body had attacked.

With Arab spears raining down on them, many members of the regiment were struck down. The British fought with determination, but the Arabs attacked relentlessly. The soldiers held their nerve and calmly returned fire. Their discipline inflicted over a thousand casualties while the British forces only suffered seventy deaths and 136 wounded.

When the Second Boer War broke out in 1899, the Berkshires were in South Africa and remained there for the duration of the conflict, fighting in several engagements. During the First World War the regiment raised sixteen battalions and lost 7,140 soldiers. The regiment received fifty-five battle honours. The 1st and 2nd Battalions were engaged in major actions on the Western Front. The 1st Battalion fought in battles at Mons, Marne, Aisne, Ypres, Festubert, Loos, Delville Wood, Ancre, Cambrai, St Quentin, Bapaume, Arras, the Second Battle of Bapaume, the Battle of Havrincourt, Canal du Nord, and the Battle of the Selle. While the 2nd Battalion fought in battles at Neuve Chapelle, Aubers, Albert, Arleux, Pilkem, St Quentin, Rosieres, and Aisne.

Further reforms changed the regiment's title in 1920; it became the Royal Berkshire Regiment (Princess Charlotte of Wales's). In 1959, defence cuts saw the regiment amalgamated with the Wiltshire Regiment (Duke of Edinburgh's) to form the Duke of Edinburgh's Royal Regiment (Berkshire and Wiltshire). In 1994, following amalgamations with the Gloucestershire Regiment, they became the Royal Gloucestershire, Berkshire, and Wiltshire Regiment. Finally, in 2007, they joined the Devonshire and Dorset Regiment, the Light Infantry, and the Royal Green Jackets to form the Rifles.

Britain's highest and most prestigious military award for valour 'in the presence of the enemy' is the Victoria Cross and Berkshire claims eleven recipients among the men of its regiment and residents of the county. Additionally, the cemeteries of Berkshire hold a further fourteen recipients of the award, but only two holders of the VC were born and buried in Berkshire. Both men were born in Reading: Trooper Frederick William Owen Potts, a private in the Berkshire Yeomanry who first came to public notice in 1913 when he saved a five-year-old boy from drowning in the River Thames, and Sir Charles Russell, 3rd Baronet, a brevet major in the Grenadier Guards.

Russell fought in the Crimean War (1853–56) at the siege and capture of Sebastopol and the battles of Alma, Balaclava and Inkerman. It was at Inkerman on 5 November 1854 that Russell won his VC, recapturing a defensive area known as the Sandbag Battery.

Above left: Second World War period cap badge.

Above right: Trooper Potts VC.

The battle lasted six hours, during which time it changed hands seven times. Conditions were appalling and the hand-to-hand fighting was bloody and intense. On one occasion, Russell volunteered to dislodge a party of Russians from the battery if anyone would follow him. A sergeant and two privates volunteered, then others followed. They met fierce resistance and several times seemed to be on the point of annihilation, but their skill with the bayonet eventually brought success. Russell fought with great valour, narrowly avoiding being bayoneted. Having killed several Russians in one single combat, he wrenched a rifle out of the grasp of a powerful Russian, turning it against him. For his many acts of bravery during the recapture of the battery, he was awarded the VC. In total, nineteen VCs were awarded during the battle.

During the First World War Trooper Potts saw active service in Gallipoli, Turkey. He was awarded the VC for his action during the Battle of Scimitar Hill when, having charged forward 1,200 feet, a bullet struck his thigh. Severely wounded, he lay in a patch of scrub among his dead comrades before spotting Reading-born Arthur Andrews alive but riddled with bullets and severely wounded, unable to move.

Attempting to reach him, a second bullet struck Pott's ear. After twenty-four hours in the heat and cold of no-man's land, realising help was not coming, Pott's began crawling back towards their lines, pulling Andrews behind him. After forty-eight hours they reached safety.

Pott's citation reads, 'For most conspicuous bravery and devotion to a wounded comrade in the Gallipoli Peninsula. Although himself severely wounded in the thigh in the attack on "Hill 70" on 21 August 1915, he remained out over 48 hours under the Turkish trenches with a private of his Regiment who was severely wounded and unable to move, although he could himself have returned to safety. Finally, he fixed a shovel to the equipment of his wounded comrade, and, using this as a sledge, he dragged him back over 600 yards to our lines, though fired at by the Turks on the way. He reached our trenches at about 9.30 p.m. on 23rd August.'

Both survived the war. A monument near Reading Crown Court commemorates Pott's heroism, together with a memorial to 426 men of the Berkshire Yeomanry who died in the Boer War and the two world wars. In Reading, Frederick has a road named after him – 'Trooper Potts Way' – close to Reading station, and a Government VC Paving Stone outside the gates of Forbury Gardens.

Thatcham commemorates three VC recipients from three different wars. Lance Corporal William House was serving with Royal Berkshire Regiment in South Africa during the Second Boer War. On 2 August 1900, during an attack on Mosilikatse Nek, William rushed out from cover while under fierce enemy fire to pick up and retrieve a wounded sergeant. William became pinned down under heavy fire. He instructed comrades not to come to his help and eventually carried the sergeant back to safety, becoming gravely wounded in the process. He received his VC from King Edward VII, in London on 24 October 1902. He died on 28 February 1912, aged thirty-two, while cleaning his rifle at Shaft Barracks, Dover.

In 1915, Second Lieutenant Alexander Buller Turner, of the 3rd (Reserve) Battalion, Royal Berkshire Regiment, won his VC during the First World War at the Battle of Loos, France. Alexander volunteered to lead a new bombing attack on enemy trenches when the regiment's bombers could not advance. Having made his way down the communication trench alone,

William House VC.

he relentlessly threw bombs towards the enemy with such dash and determination that the Germans retreated almost 500 feet. His action allowed the reserves to advance with slight losses. He then covered the regiment's flank as it retired, saving hundreds of lives. A German sniper shot Alexander in the stomach during the action, and he died three days later. His colleagues buried him with full military honours in Chocques Military Cemetery.

Alexander's brother, Lieutenant Colonel Victor Buller Turner, won his VC during the Second World War at El Aqqaqir, Egypt, during the Second Battle of El Alamein in 1942. Victor, commanding a battalion of the Rifle Brigade, overcame an entrenched German position. The battalion fought off a concerted counterattack by ninety enemy tanks, destroying or immobilising over fifty. During the attack the Germans reduced one of Victor's gun crews to one officer and a sergeant. Victor joined them as their loader and between them they destroyed another five tanks. Not until they had destroyed the last tank did he allow his head wound treatment. Victor died in 1972. Alexander and Victor are one of only four pairs of brothers to receive the VC.

In total, six members of the Royal Berkshire Regiment have received the Victoria Cross for outstanding bravery. In addition to Lance Corporal William House and Second Lieutenant Alexander Buller Turner, three were awarded during the Crimean War. These were to Major John August Conolly and Corporal James Owens for their actions at the Siege of Sevastopol, and to Sergeant George Walters at the Battle of Inkerman.

Newbury VC paving stones.

Lance Corporal James Welch also received a VC at Oppy, France, during the First World War when, having entered an enemy trench and killed one man during severe hand-to-hand fighting, then armed only with an empty revolver, he chased four of the enemy across the open, capturing them single-handed. Back in British trenches he repelled German counterattacks by using his machine gun with the utmost fearlessness, and more than once went into the open land, exposed to heavy fire, in search of ammunition and spare parts to keep his gun operational – once for over five hours, until wounded by a shell. James survived the war, dying on 28 June 1978 at Bournemouth.

A First World War memorial garden and commemorative stone honours Maidenhead resident and VC recipient Captain Thomas Tannatt Pryce of the Grenadier Guards for his bravery in France during the war. Awarded the Military Cross (MC) in 1914, leading an assault he entered German trenches unobserved, clearing and bombing large groups of the enemy crowded in deep dugouts. Although wounded, he saved his men in the face of overwhelming odds. In 1916, on the Somme, France, he received a bar to his MC for commanding the leading platoon during an assault with great verve to the enemy's trench, under heavy fire.

Thomas gained the VC in 1918 at Vieux-Berquin, France. He led two platoons in a successful attack on a village beating off four enemy attacks during the day. By evening the enemy had advanced to within 180 feet of his trench. Spurring the men on he led a bayonet charge driving them back 300 feet. With only seventeen men left and no ammunition, he led a second bayonet charge and was last seen engaged in a fierce hand-to-hand fighting against overwhelming odds. His body was never recovered.

Captain Thomas Tannatt Pryce.

5. Wings Over Berkshire

Berkshire has a long association with the nation's aviation industry. Despite this, little remains of the airfields and factories that forged that history. Its heritage, though, remains, revealing a rich and diverse connectivity to Britain's military aviation.

Royal Flying Corps (RFC) aircrew training in 1914 was inadequate because aviation itself was still in its infancy. The RFC had only been in existence for two years, and adequate teaching methods had not yet evolved. A pilot certificate granted by the Royal Aero Club of United Kingdom was all a person needed to become a military pilot and would become a major reason for the initial lack of any effective and co-ordinated training arrangements in the RFC.

In December 1915, with the First World War escalating, the RFC realised the need for dedicated schools to train the large numbers of pilots and airmen needed to meet the demands of a long war. Needing trained instructors, the War Office commandeered several buildings around Reading and at Reading University College for their School of Instruction.

The aircrew casualty rates of 1915, before the start of serious air combat, had been bearable; however, during 1916 losses became unsustainable. Needing to rapidly deliver a new initial training course for future pilots and observers, the RFC disbanded the School of Instruction at Reading on 27 October 1916, replacing it with the No. 1 School of Military Aeronautics. This transformed the college into a cosmopolitan training school for cadet pilots, and observers from across Britain, India, Commonwealth, and allied countries. At the same time, No. 2 school of Military Aeronautics was set up at Pembroke, Brasenose, Christ Church, Corpus Christi, Exeter, Jesus, Lincoln, and Queens colleges in Oxford.

Civilians and non-commissioned ranks volunteering from the army would first join an RFC Cadet Wing. Trainees underwent a two-month basic training course in military knowledge, drill, discipline, care of firearms, machine-gun use, topography, military law, and morse code. Aviation-related coursework included lectures and demonstrations on airframes and aero engines. At the end of the course they took a physical examination, which included balance and coordination tests. If they passed, the trainees put a white band around their caps, signifying they were now Flight Cadets.

Successful candidates initially attended either No. 1 or No. 2 School of Military Aeronautics, alongside officers transferring from the army. Together they trained in flight theory, aeroplane rigging, aero engines, artillery observation, map reading, and signalling.

The Reading school's headquarters were in Yeomanry House, with most lessons taught at Wantage Hall. Cadets were billeted in bell tents with wooden floors, until the RFC requisitioned accommodation in the town. They received advanced military training in drill, physical training, military law, map reading, photography, reconnaissance,

Wantage Hall, Reading University.

and signalling. One building commandeered by the government for training was the Co-Operative Wholesale Society (CWS) Preserve Works and Jam Factory Berkley Avenue. Although construction of their factory was completed in 1916, no floors or machinery had been installed thanks to a shortage of glass and sugar caused by 'the war effort'. Aircraft construction and RFC cadet training occupied large parts of the empty factory buildings. Cadets took a four-week course in artillery spotting, wireless operation, photography, machine-gun instruction, knowledge of engines, instruments and basic rigging, aviation theory, navigation, map reading, and combined infantry co-operation.

Practical lessons took place on the playing fields alongside Elmhurst Road, where cadets used wingless fuselages for cockpit familiarisation. At Upper Redlands Road, near Wantage Hall, instructors placed old aircraft fuselages in tree canopies, below which they laid out battlefield facsimiles to practise observation and recognition skills. This course should have lasted two months, but the demand was so urgent in France it was often reduced to five or six weeks.

During 1916, the first group of thirty civilian women arrived at the school to train as aircraft fitters and riggers. An armed escort chaperoned them during their training on the

Cadets billeted in bell tents. (MoBA)

Pilot instruction within the 'Jam Factory'. (MoBA)

Wingless fuselage. (MoBA)

Tree canopy, Observation Training. (MoBA)

Mock-trench system, Observation Training. (MoBA)

Compass Training. (MoBA)

Wantage Hall Fields and their physical activities, and placed hessian screens around the tennis courts to protect them from the prying eyes of cadets.

Cadets had to complete a minimum of twenty-five hours elementary flight training on both dual- and solo-control machines, followed by thirty-five hours' flying time showing proficiency in cross-country and formation flying, reconnaissance work and gunnery. Their final training at specialist schools varied in length and content according to their specific role and command destination – e.g., fighter, army co-operation, bomber or maritime. Once trained, a process that took on average eleven months, the RFC awarded cadets with their coveted pilot 'Wings' and observer's badges.

With no end in sight, the war was a tremendous strain on military aviation, and in 1917 the RFC separated the technical and practical skills of aviation, creating an additional School of Technical Training at Coley Park Aerodrome. Fighters defending London against bombing from Zeppelin airships and Gotha G. V heavy bombers of the Imperial German Air Service also used Coley Park Aerodrome.

Among the 10,000 cadets to pass through the RFC No. 1 School, was author William Earl Johns. He drew inspiration from his time and experiences as a cadet to create his now famous series of 'Biggles' adventures books. In all, a total of 112 Russians and one Japanese airmen, Fusao Ohara, known as Harry O'Hara, were cadets at Reading.

This was first published in 1934.

Tokyo-born Harry joined the Indian Army's 34th Sikh Pioneers, serving on the Western Front in 1914. He joined the Middlesex Regiment in December 1915 and returned to France in August 1916, where, wounded during an attack on the enemy, he earned the Military Medal. In March 1917, he transferred to the RFC as a second-class air mechanic and trained at the No. 1 School of Military Aeronautics. Harry then attended the London and Provincial flying school in Edgeware, where he qualified as a pilot and was promoted to sergeant. The RFC posted Harry to France, where on 1 June 1918 he was wounded in the jaw in aerial combat. Barely conscious, he safely landed his machine, and following many months of treatment was discharged from the RFC.

The Second World War airfields of Berkshire played a significant role, but today few tangible remains exist – their stories consigned to the pages of history and reference books. What does remain highlights the county's wartime aviation heritage.

Twenty-one airfields were operational in Berkshire during the height of the Second World War, but only Welford remains functional. Despite their distance from the main aerial battlefields across Britain's southern coastlines and the skies of Europe, they played important roles in training bomber crews, glider forces and paratroopers, all pivotal in the preparations for D-Day – the Battle of Normandy. They enabled Transport Command to perform an invaluable service, ferrying aircraft from local factories to operational units around the UK, and provided general air transport duties, and sites for the manufacture, production, and testing of aircraft.

Harry Fusao O'Hara. (MoBA)

The US Army's 101st Airborne Division and the United States Army Air Force (USAAF) used several Royal Air Force (RAF) airfields in Berkshire during the war. Aldermaston was the base for the USAAF's D-Day gliders and Greenham Common housed the USAAF's 26th Mobile Reclamation and Repair Squadron (Heavy). The latter produced over 400 CG-4A Waco gliders needed for Operation Albany – the US airborne phase of Operation Overlord. On 6 June 1944, C-47 Douglas Sky trains towing Waco gliders transported soldiers of the US Army's 101st and 82nd Airborne Division into battle in France during Operation Overlord. Transports supported ninety aircraft from airfields in Berkshire that delivered the first waves of paratroopers from the American 101st Airborne Division during the early hours of D-Day. Later the USAAF used them again to transport troops to the Netherlands during Operation Market Garden in September 1944.

Greenham Common was also home to two American fighter groups: the 354th flying P-51 Mustangs and the 368th who flew P-47 Thunderbolts. The USAAF utilised Welford for troop transportation and today it remains in operational use by the United States Air Force as an ammunition compound, the largest in Western Europe.

The RAF used other fields. Abingdon became a Transport Command, and home to the Army's No. 1 Parachute Training School. Designated 'Emergency Landing Grounds', Bray Court, Maidenhead, Bush Barn, Great Shefford, Winkfield, Henley-on-Thames 'Crazies Farm', and Waltham St Lawrence had their runways widened and extended in length to allow damaged bombers returning from operations over Germany to land.

The USAAF used airfields such as Kingston Bagpuize to overhaul and refurbish aeroplanes for maintenance and making modifications to their bombers. Many airfields were used by aircraft manufacturers for the production, assembling and testing of aircraft.

In 1943, Vickers-Armstrong used Aldermaston as an assembly plant to produce Spitfires, while at Woodley, between 1939 and 1945, the Miles Aircraft Factory produced 5,000 aircraft, trainers, and ancillary planes, and conducted maintenance and overhaul work on them. The government created several 'Shadow Factories' – duplicated facilities or extensions to existing facilities under the direct control of parent companies. Shadow Factories came from the Shadow Scheme, a plan devised in 1935 by the government to meet the urgent need for military aircraft, vehicles, and weapons in the buildup to the Second World War. The government tasked motor car companies with producing military equipment, alongside their regular production, so if war broke out, the new factories or their extensions could at once switch to full production.

Following heavy bombing across the south of England, at Portsmouth and Southampton the government created nine new factories. Three were in Reading, at Vincent's Garage, Station Road, Great Western Motors, Vastern Road, and a factory in Star Road, Caversham, where they produced Spitfire fuselages, wings, and engine parts. These factories transported aviation components to Henley and Aldermaston airfields, where workers assembled them for combat.

Newbury furnituremakers Elliott's also played a vital role as a 'Secret Factory', producing aircraft parts for the Spitfire, Mosquito fighter bomber, and the Airspeed Oxford and Horsa Gliders. Elliott's built one third of all the Horsa Gliders made, many of these were used by the Allies during their invasion of France in 1944.

58

In 1938, Hawker Aircraft Ltd opened an aircraft factory and airfield on Parlaunt Farm, Langley to develop and produce Hurricane, Tornado, Typhoon, Tempest and Fury fighter planes, along with the Sea Fury and the General Aircraft Hamilcar X tank-carrying glider, all making maiden flights from the airfield. The Battle of Britain Memorial Flight includes the 'Last of Many', the last Hawker Hurricane produced at Langley. In Langley and Woodley, like other villages, roads and residential areas reflect this heritage, recognising manufacturers, Miles Way (Miles Aircraft Ltd) aircraft Spitfire Close, Hurricane Way and

Above and below: Wokingham signs.

Hurricane Court; and individuals, The Bader Way in honour of Group Captain Douglas Bader, who having lost both legs in a flying accident at Woodley became a flying hero of the Second World War. All reflecting their proud association with the county's aviation heritage.

In 1940, the Luftwaffe destroyed Vickers-Armstrong's main Wellington Bomber factory at Brooklands, Surrey. The government commandeered Smith's Lawn airfield, Windsor Great Park, which became shrouded in secrecy during the war when Vickers-Armstrong created a new Wellington Bomber assembly plant there. Code named 'Vaxi' by Vickers-Armstrong, the factory spanned two brick-built hangers where they constructed several high-altitude versions of their Wellington Bomber. The airfield also accommodated the USAAF 316th Squadron, 31st Transport Group and consequently the UC-78 Bobcat, UC-64 Norseman, and L-5 Sentinel planes were a common sight over Windsor during the war.

At Newbury, Stradlings Garage, Pass Garage, Nias Garages, Ventures Bus Works, Mill Lane Works, Shaw Works, Baughurst Garage, and Elliott's were all requisitioned to produce parts for Walrus Amphibian aeroplanes, Wellington Bombers and Spitfires. These were machine shops, producing small utility parts, such as nuts, bolts, and washers.

Vickers Wellington Bombers flew from airfields at Hampstead Norris and, during the latter part of the war, its satellite station Harwell. The RAF used these airfields as glider training stations to prepare for the Normandy D-Day landings; the first glider-borne troops of the main force were from Harwell. Both airfields also ferried airborne troops for Operation Market Garden – the abortive attempt to capture the Rhine bridge at Arnhem. The Special Operations Executive also used Harwell briefly for operations between July and September 1944.

The RAF set up flight training schools at Shellingford, Theale and Woodley and used Watchfield for Blind Landing Training. They also created a School of Air Traffic Control there, and after the war the army used it as a practice drop zone for parachute training and vehicle air drops. The No. 16 Parachute Heavy Drop company (RAOC) formed there in 1961.

At Crookham Common, the US Army Air Corps requisitioned the aerodrome as an airfield in early 1941. In the build-up to D-Day it became a Glider Assembly Camp for the 101st Airborne Division before they transferred to Greenham Common, where the USAAF deployed them in Normandy.

While most of the military airfields and establishments no longer remain. Berkshire's military aviation legacy exists through its heritage in the stories of the people, places and events that shaped the county's history, and in the few buildings, museum artifacts and tributes that can be seen today.

6. Unsung Heroes of the Air

On 28 June 1919, the Treaty of Versailles ended war between Germany and the Allied powers, and among the restrictions placed on Germany were the limitations on its military capacity and capability. When the German president, Paul von Hindenburg, appointed Adolf Hitler as Chancellor in 1932, Hitler immediately began secretly expanding Germany's military capabilities. In 1935, he publicly denounced the treaty, reinforced its western frontier, and rearmed the nation. By 1936 he had created a force of 2,500 planes and an army of 300,000 men, which, through compulsory military conscription, increased to 600,000 by 1938, and to 1.5 million by 1939.

Hitler continued to flout the treaty's restrictions in 1936, creating a fascist coalition with Italy and an anti-communist alliance with Japan. The British and French governments' response was a fatal policy of appeasement that allowed Hitler to illegally remilitarise the Rhineland and annex Austria, in a move that would pave the way for Germany's conquest of Czechoslovakia and Poland.

Expecting an armed conflict with Germany, the director of British Airways Overseas Corporation (BAOC), Gerald d'Erlanger CBE, wrote to the Air Ministry on 24 March 1938 suggesting that a ferry pool comprising civilian and commercial pilots be set up from pilots unable to meet military requirements for flying. If required, these pilots could relieve pressure on the RAF by transporting, supplies, dispatches, mail, the wounded,

ATA side cap badge.

medical officers, and dignitaries around the United Kingdom. Besides pilots, a ground school of instructors, engineers, crash rescue teams, meteorological officers, motor transport drivers, nurses and doctors, and administration staff were also needed. Air cadets could be employed as messengers and auxiliary crew members.

The Air Ministry did not accept the suggestion, but when war broke out in August 1939 they created RAF ferry pools under d'Erlanger's control. He employed male pilots from BAOC.

In October, the Air Member for Supply and Organisation (AMSO), Air Vice Marshal W. L. Welsh, took operational control of the ferry pools, and posted all pilots fit to fly to combat units in the RAF Reserve (RAFR). BAOC, with d'Erlanger in command, kept control of the administration of the ferry pools and their non-operational pilots.

Early in 1940, the Air Ministry renamed the ferry pool the Air Transport Auxiliary (ATA). Besides a transportation role, 'ferry pilots' began flying fighter, bomber, and training aircraft to and from factories, assembly plants, transatlantic delivery points, maintenance units (MUs), scrapyards, active service squadrons, training units, and airfields.

On 22 July 1941, the Air Ministry placed the ATA under the control of Lord Beaverbrook's Ministry of Aircraft Production (MAP). Although control of the ATA shifted, the administration continued to be under the staff led by d'Erlanger.

The increasing demands, combined with a shortfall in pilots, created a unique opportunity for the ATA to employ women to ferry military planes for the first time in aviation history. Public attitude was that aviation was an unsuitable profession for a woman and that female pilots would take flying roles away from men. That did not

Sir Gerard d'Erlanger.

stop d'Erlanger employing Pauline Gower, a commercial pilot with over 2,000 hours flight experience, as the commandant for the women's section of the ATA.

The ATA set up its headquarters at the Royal Air Force, White Waltham airfield, Maidenhead, Berkshire. White Waltham was No. 1 Ferry Pool, the first and most prominent of fourteen flight pilot pools created across the country. By the end of the war the ATA operated from twenty-two pools. An Air Movements Flight section was established at White Waltham in 1941, responsible for ferrying VIPs and transporting vital supplies, medicines, and vaccines from the UK to Europe. During their return trips they would convey returning prisoners of war and Allied wounded in need of hospitalisation.

Several pools were near aircraft factories, which made them targets for German bombers. The nearest factories to No. 1 Ferry Pool were at Brooklands (Vickers-Armstrong), Langley (Hawker) and Woodley (Miles).

Initially Commander Gower only recruited to White Waltham female pilots who had over 250 flying hours. As demand for the service continued to increase, this was reduced to 150 and then fifty flying hours, and finally she created a program of in-house flight training for pilots which attracted female volunteers from the Commonwealth, USA, and Netherlands.

The average age of female pilots in the ATA was twenty-seven. The youngest and the oldest members were both South Africans. Dolores Theresa Sorour from Pretoria received her flying licence aged fifteen, and by seventeen she had become the first woman to perform a parachute jump in South Africa. She moved to the United Kingdom in 1938 and was twenty when she joined.

Pauline Gower. (NPG)

ATA pilot and engineer badge.

Grace Brown from Natal became the oldest pilot at forty-three, when she joined during the British Expeditionary Force's evacuation from Dunkirk. The first woman to fly to the front, she stunned RAF pilots by landing at an airfield in Nantes France on 18 May 1940, with a consignment of blood in the middle of a German attack.

The RAF restricted female pilots, later dubbed 'Attagirls', to flying trainers and transport aircraft, but it soon became apparent that female pilots were every bit as skilful as their male counterparts and could not only fly the same planes but would also be the first women in Britain to get equal pay. It was dangerous work, with mechanical failure, weather, bad luck, and enemy aircraft presenting real dangers every time they took a plane to the sky. In all, 168 women served with the ATA. Fifteen lost their lives in the air over Britain.

Of note to Berkshire, the first Berkshire ATA fatality was Second Officer Joy Davison, a Canadian-born British pilot who gained her flying certificate aged twenty. Having worked as a mechanic at several national air manufacturers, she became the nation's first female director of a plane company – Utilities Airways Ltd. Joy joined the ATA at White Waltham on 1 July 1940, only to die seven days later during a training flight in which she and her instructor, Sergeant Edgar Francis L'Estrange, succumbed to carbon monoxide poisoning, causing her plane to spiral out of control at RAF Uphaven, Wiltshire.

The cemetery at All Saints' Church, Maidenhead, holds the graves of twenty ATA pilots. Their composition reflects the diversity of the ATA and their ferry pilots. Among their number are two Americans, two South Africans, one Polish, one Australian and one New Zealander.

Above left: Dolores Theresa Sorour. (NPG)

Above right: Grace Brown.

Left: Joy Davison.

Above: ATA Graves, All Saints' Cemetery.

Right: First Officer Rosamund
King Everard-Steenkamp.

Second Officer Antoni Henryk Gosiewski.

The first pilot from White Waltham to die in service was Second Officer Henry Edward Taylor, who was flying an Avro 641 Commodore. This was one of only six built during the 1930s and pressed into service by Fairey Aviation Co. Ltd at White Waltham. Taylor crashed while approaching the airfield on 10 August 1941, sustaining multiple fractures and chemical burns, and died in hospital a week later.

On 15 March 1942, Cadet Betty Sayer was one of four ATA members onboard a Fairchild Argus light transporter returning to White Waltham. It flew into foul weather during the approach, the engine stalled and the plane crashed onto a bungalow in Smithfield Road. The occupant of the bungalow survived, being blown out the building when the plane struck, as was a neighbour in an adjoining property, who also survived; her son was rescued from their front room. The plane's petrol tank exploded, seriously injuring twenty-six civilians trying to rescue passengers from the wreckage. Betty died alongside Flying Officer Graham Lever and Third Officer Bridget Hill. Third Officer Pamela Duncan survived.

A mid-air collision killed ATA First Officer John Erickson (USA) on 9 May 1942 just after taking off from White Waltham. Another Blenheim struck Erickson's Bristol Blenheim light bomber and severed the tail of Erickson's plane. He crashed in a field just off Woodlands Park Avenue; the other plane, piloted by First Officer Robert Pavey, crashed behind a bungalow near Cox Green, killing him and two other ATA members.

A month later, South African-born Third Officer Joan Esther Marshall died on 20 June 1942 when her Miles Master two-seat monoplane advanced trainer stalled during a turn to approach the runway. It spun towards the ground and crashed into a garden in Maidenhead. Members of the ATA buried Joan with full military honours and Gower was among her pallbearers.

New Zealander Second Officer Jane Winstone began flying solo aged seventeen, and became New Zealand's youngest female pilot, gaining her pilot's licence in August 1931. On 10 February 1944, Jane was ferrying a Spitfire across Shropshire from Tong to Cosforde. The engine twice partially failed before it completely stopped working and the aircraft stalled, spinning into the ground 2 miles north of Tong airfield.

Right: Jane Winstone.

Below: Australian Thomas Bray and American John Erickson.

Berkshire's airfields were home to many women pilots who before the war were famous in their own rights. Pioneer Amy Johnson, a celebrated solo long-distance pilot and record holder was a frequent visitor to Woodley and White Waltham and died in ATA service in 1941. As did aircraft designer Maxine Blossom Miles and flight test engineer air-racing pilot and lady's world-speed record holder Lettice Curtis. In June 1941, famous American aviatrix Jacqueline Cochran became the first woman to fly a bomber across the Atlantic Ocean when she flew a Lockheed Hudson light bomber to Scotland as part of the 'Lend and Lease' American Wings for Britain programme. She joined the ATA and became a flight captain. She selected twenty-five American female pilots to join the ATA at White Waltham in 1942, referring to them as 'Attagirls'. She returned to the states in 1943 to form the Women's Airforce Service Pilots (WASP), for which she became the first civilian woman to receive the Distinguished Service Medal.

During the war, the ATA's total pilot complement comprised 1,152 men and 166 women from twenty-eight countries. They flew in excess of 415,000 hours, ferrying over 309,000 people in 147 different types of aircraft ranging from light training aircraft to fighter planes and bombers. It is worth noting the ATA recruited over a 1,000 pilots rejected by the RAF for being too old or unfit for service because of some physical disability, giving rise to the term Ancient and Tattered Airmen (ATA) for the male pilots. Of the 166 female pilots fifteen died on active service.

Thirty-six pilots, among them two women, received certificates of commendation from the British government. Four women pilots – Pauline Gower, Margot Gore, Joan Hughes,

Jacqueline Cochran (NAR RAD).

ATA pilots, 1942. (PdWC)

and Rosemary Rees – were awarded MBEs (Members of the British Empire). Gower did not live long enough to indulge her passion for flying, dying in 1947 shortly after giving birth to twin boys.

In the lead up to D-Day, the Air Ministry designated White Waltham and Aston Down, Gloucestershire, as ATA Invasion Pools, delivering fighters to front-line squadrons. After D-Day, the Invasion Pool pilots ferried operational service aircraft throughout western and southern Europe and the Mediterranean. White Waltham pilots also provided support during the ill-fated attempt to capture the bridge at Arnhem in the Netherlands, in September 1944.

Following Germany's unconditional surrender on 5 May 1945, the Air Ministry told the ATA that their services would no longer be needed on 2 June 1945, and that they would be fully decommissioned by 31 December. The RAF offered some male pilots commissions with the RAF as ferry pilots, but no provision existed or allowed the transfer of women pilots into the RAF. Upon leaving, Gerard d'Erlanger presented each ATA member with a blue and gold Certificate of Service and a personal letter of thanks.

The Aston Invasion Pool was the first to be decommissioned and, when Japan surrendered on 15 August, the date for full decommissioning was moved forward to 30 November. By the end of September, however, all pools had been closed, leaving only No. 1 Ferry Pool ATA and the administrative headquarters at White Waltham open.

In what was the only opportunity for the public to see the work of the ATA, they held a special Air Pageant on 29 September 1945 at White Waltham. Lord Beaverbrook, Minister of Aircraft Production, gave a rousing speech to the 12,000 members of public in which he declared, 'the ATA had written a splendid chapter in British history'.

White Waltham Second World War blister hangar.

White Waltham Second World War ATA clubhouse.

The pageant included a memorable collection of Allied and German aircraft, including a V-1 flying bomb, aero engines, an anti-aircraft gun, and searchlight complete with crew and featured a flying display by test pilots – ATA pilots did not hold appropriate licences to perform in flying displays. They did, however, operate an air taxi service to convey pilots to their starting points.

Several types of aircraft were used, but the Avro Anson proved most suitable, and so it was apt that the pageant's last flight into White Waltham was an Avro Anson taxi flight returning pilots who had ferried the very last ATA aircraft.

The pageant raised money for the ATA's benevolent fund, supporting widows and orphans of the 174 members who lost their lives. Lord Beaverbrook gave their fund a much-needed boost when he presented a cheque for £5,000 from the aircraft companies the ATA had served during the war. The airfield remained in RAF hands until 1982, when it was bought by the current owners and is now home to a flying school and long-standing aero club.

White Waltham air pageant, 1945. (JT)

7. Leading the Way

Berkshire has played a big part in producing military leaders across three services. This chapter looks at the history, traditions and heritage created by the Royal Military College; its successor, the Royal Military Academy (the Shop) Sandhurst; the Royal Air Force's Staff College and its successor, the Joint Services Command, Bracknell; the Nautical College, Pangbourne. All of whom have produced famous and influential military leaders and important personalities.

Royal Military College at Sandhurst

It was during the disastrous campaigns experienced during the French Revolutionary War (1792–1802) that one of the finest cavalry commanders of his generation, Major-General John Gaspard Le Marchant, identified numerous deficiencies in the British cavalry's equipment and training.

Returning to Britain, Le Marchant was determined to improve the situation. A superb mounted swordsman developed a system of swordsmanship and designed a new cavalry sabre, which were adopted by the army. Le Marchant toured Britain teaching his system, which greatly influenced the efficient functioning of the Army. Le Marchant suggested a new system of military instruction for training infantry and cavalry officers, like that provided for artillery and engineering officers at the Royal Military Academy at Woolwich, London.

Major-General John Gaspard Le Marchant.

After overcoming considerable opposition on the grounds of cost, Parliament provided a grant in 1802 of £30,000 to establish a Royal Military College at High Wycombe and a Royal Military College at Great Marlow, Buckinghamshire. The colleges provided instruction to serving officers in the roles and responsibilities of being a staff officer, and the schooling of gentlemen cadets before they gained an officer's commission.

Ten years later the schools merged, transferring to the purpose-built Royal Military College at Sandhurst, where Le Marchant's role in establishing the military schools is commemorated today. One of the college's VIP dining rooms is named after him and displays objects relating to him.

Until 1870 cavalry and infantry officers bought their first commissions and subsequent promotions up to the rank of colonel. This system of 'purchasing' a commission required the officer to produce evidence of having received a gentleman's education. If the regimental colonel approved the request, then the officer would have to produce a sum of money dictated by Parliament relevant to the rank required. This would also show an individual's financial standing in society. Colonels offered officers promotions on a seniority basis. An officer could not purchase a 'staff appointment' (responsibility for the unit's administrative, operational, and logistical needs) and would revert to the rank of his last purchased commission when this tenure was over.

When an officer left the army, the military refunded their last payment for a commission, providing a substantial amount of capital to invest elsewhere. The system was open to abuse, with wealthy officers bribing juniors not to take promotions, but it

Cadets at Sandhurst, *c.* 1812. (NAM)

also allowed officers to command regiments in their twenties while they had their health and fitness.

Officers entered Sandhurst as cadets aged fifteen. Besides military laws and etiquette, instructors at the college applied their own petty rules, which caused discontent among the cadets and the college soon gained a reputation for disorderly conduct. The War Office raised the entrance age to seventeen, but standards and behaviour continued to decline, with rioting and bullying being commonplace. In 1862, 1,000 disillusioned cadets withstood a three-day siege in an earthwork built at the college for fortifications training. The siege only broke when the college's commander-in-chief, Prince George, the Duke of Cambridge, intervened personally.

The college abolished the purchase system of promotion in 1870 and introduced a competitive academic entrance examination that restricted entrants to boys from families with wealth or military connections and influence. Students were referred to as gentlemen cadets and were not subject to military law. Except for a few scholarships, families paid for tuition fees, uniforms, books and boarding, and each student wore the uniform of a junior officer of the day minus any badges of rank. Successful completion of training and exams would enable cadets to receive a commission as a second lieutenant.

This system remained in place until 1939. When war broke out the college closed, senior cadets took commissions and junior cadets went into the newly created Officer Cadet Training Unit (OCTU). This unit comprised two branches, 101 Royal Armoured Corps OCTU who remained at Sandhurst and 161 Infantry OCTU, who moved to Mons barracks, Aldershot.

Cadets bridge building at Sandhurst, c. 1911. (NAM)

The War Office introduced a new training programme for potential officers in 1947, which provided three routes into the army with training appropriate for the length of service. Those entering on national service (two years) attended a four-month course at the Officer Cadet School (OCS), Eaton Hall, Cheshire. Volunteers joining on a short-service commission (four years) attended a six-month course at the OCS Mons Barracks, Aldershot, and men joining the regular army attended a twenty-four-month course at the renamed Royal Military Academy Sandhurst (RMAS).

At the RMAS, cadets underwent a two-year rolling programme of military and academic training for officers from all branches of the army. The training focused on developing the cadet's leadership skills in line with the academy's motto 'Serve to Lead'. Adventure and outward-bound training skills, along with all major sporting activities featured in the syllabus, as did recreational pursuits like yachting and flying. The Literary Society became known as the 'Polished Bun Club', and the Parachuting Club 'The Edward Bear Club'.

Before the government abolished national service in 1960, they combined Mons OCTU and Eaton Hall OCTU to form the Mons Officer Cadet School (Mons OCU). OCU became responsible for training all short-service officer cadets.

Another review of officer cadet training came in 1972. When the Mons OCU closed, the RMAS reorganised its training for student officers and officer cadets, including regulars, short service, and territorials. The college ensured all officer entrants underwent a six-month intense course, at which point the short service officers left the academy.

Regular officers also left and, having completed a period of regimental duties, returned to RMAS to Old College for a modified course of academic training. Students focused on politics, international affairs, and war studies. Cadets also received training tailored to their chosen military profession – chaplain, medic, lawyer and education.

Over the next twenty-five years the academy underwent many changes to meet organisational needs. In 1984, the army allowed female officers to train at the RMAS, and in 2015 Colonel Lucy Giles became the first female commander at Sandhurst. Before then, women had their own training college, the Women's Royal Army Corps College, in Camberley. Until 1992, three separate courses were delivered: the first for male graduates, the second for male non-graduates and the third for female cadets. This non-standardised system of training had become divisive and a source of unhealthy rivalry. This changed in 1992 when the RMAS standardised the training across the board with a new 'Commissioning Course'.

The Old College contains many historic buildings, monuments, and memorials. Of interest is the statue of Louis-Napoleon, Prince Imperial, a gentleman cadet at Woolwich RMA (1872–1875) who declined his commission and met his death in 1879 while on a reconnaissance patrol in the Zulu War. Another statue is a large charging bronze boar, the insignia of XXX Corps led by Lieutenant General Sir Brian Horrocks during the Second World War. While in Germany, one of General Horrocks' staff officers spotted a large bronze statue of a seated boar in the grounds of a country house and removed it as a trophy of war. Horrocks had the boar placed on a plinth marked with the corps' battle honours, and on the eve of relinquishing command it was unveiled outside XXX

XXX Corps boar statue.

Sandhurst's Sovereign's Parade.

Headquarters in Nienburg, Germany. Their charging boar insignia was replaced with one at rest, having completed its duties. The statue was moved by the army to the Staff College in 1958.

The Royal Air Force Staff College

The Staff College has always been an important part of the Royal Air Force (RAF). Between 1945 and 1996 the RAF equivalent to RMAS was the RAF Staff College, responsible for training staff officers in the administration of staff and related policy and procedural matters. Located in the Victorian villa of Ramslade House, Broad Lane, Bracknell, it also accommodated the headquarters for the RAF's Second Tactical Air Force from 1943 to 1945.

The RAF Staff College first opened at Andover, Hampshire, on 3 April 1922. Courses comprised twenty student officers and lasted twelve months. It remained in this format until the outbreak of the Second World War in September 1939. To meet the increased need for staff-trained officers, courses were shortened to a three-month duration. The third course was suspended following the fall of France on 27 May 1940, with directing staff and students assuming urgent operational appointments.

Before they could restart courses, the Staff College was damaged by an enemy air attack in April 1941. They found a new home for the college at Bulstrode Park, Gerrards Cross, Buckinghamshire. Courses recommenced in January 1942 with course sizes rising to sixty students, including offices from the Royal Navy, army and Allied Forces; the duration of the course remained three months.

Ramslade House, 1936. (JT)

In 1945, the Air Ministry moved the college to Ramslade and, extending the course to a six-month duration, increased the intake to 120 student officers. Accommodation soon proved inadequate and a small wing of the college was established at Bulstrode comprising thirty-two officer students – sixteen from Allied Air Forces and sixteen from the RAF. This wing became a separate unit in 1946 and in 1948 moved back to Andover as the Royal Air Force College (Andover). It comprised forty student officers, with twenty drawn from Allied Air Forces and the rest from the RAF.

At Ramsdale the main staff course comprised ninety-six students from the RAF, army and Royal Navy, with representatives from the United States Air Force, United States Navy, and old Commonwealth Air Forces. They returned the duration of both courses to one year.

In January 1970, the Staff College at Andover and Bracknell merged to form an enlarged college located at Bracknell, housed in the purpose-built tutorial accommodation within the grounds of Ramslade. A major review of command and staff training in 1973 led to the setting up of the Basic Staff Course (BSC) in 1974 to prepare squadron leaders for command and staff appointments appropriate to their rank.

Eight twenty-three-day BSCs were delivered a year, with up to twenty-four students on each course. The syllabus covered all forms of verbal and written communication skills, aspects of human behaviour, project control, computer applications and cost accounting principles.

To prepare officers to fill high-grade command and staff appointments, the following year the new Advanced Staff Course (ASC) was introduced. Lasting ten months, the course comprised fifty-four RAF officers and thirty-six officers from other UK Services, the Commonwealth, and foreign air forces. Selected officers received an advanced service education, the principal study area of which were staff methods, RAF and joint-service operations, logistics, strategy, and national defence and overseas theatre studies.

RAF Staff College, First Course Ramslade, 1945. (JT)

Site of Ramslade House today.

On 1 January 1997, the college closed when responsibility for RAF staff training transferred to the newly established Joint Services Command and Staff College, which remained at Ramslade House until 2000, when the Defence Academy of the United Kingdom moved it to a purpose-built facility at Watchfield, near Shrivenham, Swindon, Wiltshire. The Ministry of Defence sold Ramslade House to English Partnerships, a regeneration agency who demolished it in 2015 and replaced it with a housing development.

The Nautical College, Pangbourne

Founded by merchant tradesperson Sir Thomas Lane Devitt in 1917, the Nautical College, Pangbourne, Devitt House, was formally occupied by Clayesmore School, an independent co-educational school now located in the village of Iwerne Minster in Dorset. The purpose of the Nautical College was to prepare boys to become officers in the Merchant Navy.

Historically, naval training was undertaken onboard a ship in dry dock or moored on a river, estuary, or harbour. With Germany escalating its campaign of unrestricted submarine warfare it was considered safer to locate a nautical training college inland. The Admiralty, supportive of the college's activities, allowed students to wear naval uniform, granting them cadet status in the Royal Naval Reserve, in line with similar schools such as the Incorporated Thames Nautical Training College, HMS *Worcester*, Thames Estuary, and HMS *Conway* on the Mersey near Liverpool. These two institutions closed in 1968

Devitt House, Pangbourne College.

and 1974 respectively, as the number of young men seeking a career at sea declined, and in 1969 the Nautical College, Pangbourne, became Pangbourne College.

Following the change, Pangbourne College moved to a stronger academic programme, replacing the post of captain superintendent with a civilian head teacher. Besides normal academic subjects, the curriculum included theoretical and practical seamanship and navigation to O level and Higher National Diploma in seamanship for cadets seeking a career in the Merchant Navy. Originally the college capacity was 200 male cadets destined for service in the Merchant or Royal Navy. However, in 1996 the college became co-educational and created a junior house, increasing capacity to 430 cadets.

Pangbourne College retains several naval traditions such as referring to their boarding houses as divisions. In naval language a division is a group of ships that form part of a squadron or taskforce, bedrooms are known as cabins, the common rooms are gunrooms, kitchens are galleys, and the dining hall is the mess hall. Another legacy is its focus on waterborne activities such as rowing, which feature strongly in the college's extracurricular activities.

Although the title of cadet is no longer used, pupils continue to wear naval uniform on a daily basis, including the traditional rank slides of a Royal Navy cadet. On a daily basis pupils wear the No. 2 uniform, blue shirt and trousers/skirt, blue pullover, black socks, and shoes. At ceremonial events they wear the No. 1 uniform, a double-breasted, navy blue reefer jacket with four rows of two buttons, matching trousers/skirt, white shirt, black tie, peaked cap, black socks/tights, and black shoes.

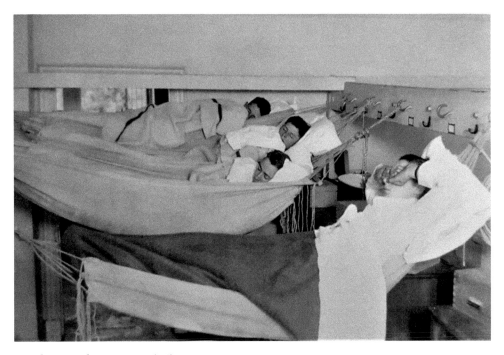

Boarders, Pangbourne, 1927. (PC)

Cadets, *c.* 1930. (PC)

Every day the college flies a Blue Ensign flag awarded by the Admiralty. Every third Sunday of the month the college holds a naval-themed parade in which pupils, accompanied by the college's marching band, march to church. The academic year concludes on Founders Day with a naval-themed ceremony, culminating in the band 'Beating the Retreat', a ceremony dating from the seventeenth century when the beating of drums and the parading of post guards at the end of the day heralded the closing of the college gates and the lowering of flags.

8. Commemoration and Remembrance

Commemoration of Britain's war dead did not develop until the end of the nineteenth century. Before then memorials were rare and dedicated to individual officers or regiments. The first large-scale construction of war memorials for the ordinary soldier came after the Second Boer War in 1899–1902, when the public, through donations and subscriptions, erected memorials in churches, churchyards, town halls and other prominent places. These memorials ranged from metal and stone plaques to statues and obelisks. The most common were brass plaques like those at Newbury Town Hall and St George's Church, Reading.

Military memorials and monuments are important heritage assets and a valuable source of historical information. The Berkshire Family History Society (BFHS) has transcribed and indexed 900 memorials across the 'old' Royal County of Berkshire, listing the names of 32,600 people. Most military monuments and memorials in Berkshire remember people, places and events associated with the First and Second World Wars, but many other conflicts are also commemorated.

From private and personal remembrance to imposing public tributes, these memorials take many forms: sculptures, crosses, obelisks, cenotaphs, columns, boards, plaques, walls, tablets, rolls of honour, books of remembrance, buildings, parks, gardens, playing fields, woodland, shelters, towers, streets, museums, galleries, and trophies of war. While it is not possible to describe each one in this chapter, I encourage the reader to contact the BFHS for further information about their locations and accessibility.

The Falkland Memorial sits at the top of Wash Common, an imposing obelisk built of grey Cornish granite it stands on the site of Newbury battlefield. Dedicated to the memory of those who died fighting for Charles I on 20 September 1643 during the First Battle of Newbury. The memorial takes its name from the secretary of state Lucius Cary, 2nd Viscount Falkland, who died during the fighting. Falkland took part in the fighting at the Siege of Gloucester in August 1643, where he behaved with manic, reckless courage, despite the pleas of his friends who feared for his state of mind. During the Battle of Newbury, Falkland was killed charging alone through a gap in a hedge lined with Parliamentarian musketeers. This action was regarded by observers as an act of suicide brought about by his despair at the horror of civil war.

The county has another large Falkland memorial in the chapel at Pangbourne College. This national memorial commemorates the courage of servicemen and women who protected the Falkland Islands sovereignty and the 255 men and three women who lost their lives during the battle to reclaim them in 1982. Claimed by British Royal Naval Captain John Byron for George III in 1765, the island's name comes from the channel of water separating the two main islands, the 'Falkland Sound'. The sound, so named in 1690 in honour of Anthony Cary, 5th Viscount of Falkland, descendant of Lucius Cary, 2nd Viscount Falkland.

Left: Falkland memorial, Newbury.

Below: Falkland memorial, Pangbourne.

Laurenthes Braag memorial.

One of Berkshire's more unusual military monuments is in the grounds of Purley Hall, Purley on Thames. Standing 720 feet to the west and set back from the water's edge amongst the shrubbery, is a rustic seat inside a knapped and knobbly flint temple, similar in style to those in the north gateway and lodges. Its open front overlooks the canal, and local tradition says it was built in 1746 to commemorate the Battle of Culloden in 1745. The Duke of Cumberland (Prince William, George II's son, and resident of Sunningdale), marched six thousand troops from Greenham to fight at the Battle of Culloden. Amongst his troops were many men from Berkshire; it is likely that the memorial honours them or a family member from Purley Hall who fought at Culloden.

On the exterior of the south wall of St Mary's Church, Reading, is a memorial to Merchantman Laurenthes Braag, who was taken prisoner in 1801 during the Battle of Copenhagen, during the Napoleonic Wars of 1803–15. Braag, with other Danish prisoners, became known as 'Gentlemen Danes' because of their upright behaviour while on parole in Reading. Braag died on 3 September 1808, aged twenty-six, a year before George III released all Danish prisoners to mark his golden jubilee. Laurenthes' friends and countrymen paid to have this memorial stone raised for him.

While several memorials across the county commemorate individuals who fought in the First War of Indian Independence (1857–58), only one, on a beautiful white marble stone in St Mary's Church, Winkfield, commemorates a casualty. Eighteen years and two months old, Ensign Edmund Cadell Scott was one of nine officers from the 28th Bengal Native Infantry murdered in their camp on 23 June 1857 at Mohumdee, Uttar Pradesh, India.

At Great Windsor, an ornate Indian kiosk of white marble with an onion dome, round arches and deep eaves sits in the grounds of Frogmore House. Captured by Lord Canning, Governor-General of India following the Siege of Lucknow, it was brought back to England where he presented it to Queen Victoria in 1858 to commemorate the end of the First Indian War of Independence.

One of the more unusual wars commemorated is the Second Opium War of 1856–60. At St John the Baptist Church, Shottesbrooke, a rare naval memorial commemorates Nicholas Vansittart. A Royal Navy captain, Nicholas was born in Shottesbrooke and died on 17 July 1859 on board HMS *Magicienne* after injuries sustained during an unsuccessful attack on the Peiho forts on the Hai River, north-eastern China. Vansittart also captained HMS *Magicienne* during the Crimean War of 1853–56. He sailed into Biorko Bay, Leningrad, Russia, and shelled infantry on the shore before sinking two ships laden with granite destined for defences at Cronstadt. Buried in the Shantung Road Cemetery, Shanghai, China, his brother officers and friends erected a tablet, decorated with leaves and an anchor, as a token of their esteem and admiration.

Berkshire's most iconic memorial is the Maiwand Lion in Forbury Gardens, Reading. Named after a small Afghanistan village, it was erected in 1866. The original colour of the lion was 'invisible green', a military colour designed to help camouflage. The colour changed over the years with varying shades of textured paint being applied to mimic a stone finish. In the early part of the twentieth century, before it's restoration in 2004, it was returned to its original colouring. Made of cast iron and weighing 16 tons, the Lion is one of the biggest cast-iron statues in the world. It commemorates the lives of 328 men of the 66th Berkshire Regiment who died on 27 July 1880 at Maiwand and Khanda during a campaign to stop Russian threats to Britain's control of India.

An army of 2,700 British and Indian troops tried to halt 12,000 Pashtun warriors led by Ayoub Khan, the brother of Afghanistan's deposed ruler, from marching on Kabul. Heavily outnumbered, the Afghans defeated the British at the Maiwand Pass but suffered high casualties – 2,750 men killed and 1,500 wounded. British and Indian forces suffered 969 soldiers killed and 177 wounded and were forced to retreat in disarray to Kandahar.

At the Rifles Berkshire and Wiltshire Museum in Salisbury are the remains of a little-known hero of the battle. Mounted on display is Bobbie, a brave mongrel dog from Reading stationed at Brock Barracks with the 2nd Battalion of the Royal Berkshire

Hero Bobby. (TRM)

Regiment. Bobbie barked defiantly at the head of the valiant troops during the battle. Wounded and having been taken prisoner, he escaped and joined the remnants of the regiment in Kandahar.

Back in England, Bobbie was presented to Queen Victoria, who having heard his story awarded him the Afghan Medal, pinning it to his collar. Bobbie died in Gosport, Hampshire, when he was run over by a hansom cab – news that deeply saddened Queen Victoria.

Men of the 66th are also remembered at the Bugle pub in Friar Street, Reading, where the uniform worn by a bugler of the 66th in Afghanistan in 1880 is depicted.

Of the tens of thousands of villages and towns in Britain, all but fifty-three 'thankful villages' lost men in the First World War. Villages who lost men from their community began creating memorials to heroes who lost their lives in the conflict. These memorials provide a noble and enduring tribute and were in the main created via special committees who raised funds, selected locations, and chose the design, decisions that were often not harmonious.

The Royal Sculpture Association set up an advisory committee in 1919 to offer advice on designs and suitable inscriptions, but there was no national instruction or restrictions on design or what materials and mediums to use. This resulted in a diverse mix of traditional monuments, such as the popular stone obelisks and crosses being erected alongside individualised memorials like buildings, gardens, and artistic works.

Inside the entrance to the Grundon Waste Management, Star lane, Knowle Hill, Reading, is an unusual roll of honour commemorating sixty-five staff of the Warner and Company Star Works' brick and tile makers. An elaborately decorated wooden plaque

Warner and Company Star Works memorial.

within an oak frame on low brick supports, it uncharacteristically celebrates the safe return of fifty-five workers and remembers nine who died.

An impressive monument to the school's old boys (OBs) who died during both world wars stands in the grounds of former Beaumont College (1861–1967), Old Windsor. Despite being one of England's smallest public schools, Beaumont's military contribution was significant. There were 110 OBs who fought in the Boer War, the largest contingent from any Catholic school or college involved in the First World War. OBs came from the British Empire and Dominions as well as France, Belgium, and America. They served in all services and ranks from general to private and naval equivalents.

The college suffered one of the highest losses, with 133 OBs dying during the First World War. The youngest was fifteen-year-old Midshipman Geoffrey Harold, who drowned in the North Sea in September 1914 when a German submarine torpedoed the Royal Navy cruiser HMS *Hogue*. Geoffrey's last act before leaping into the sea as ordered was lashing two boards together for another midshipman who could not swim. His brother Bevan died in 1918, shot down during a reconnaissance mission. Seven sets of brothers from the college died during the First World War, along with one father and son.

Other notable OBs commemorated include Lieutenant Harry Butters, who in 1915 became the first American to volunteer for the British Expeditionary Force, and Lt-General Sir George MacDonogh, who brought back the body of the 'Unknown Warrior' from Flanders for burial in Westminster Abbey in 1920. Brigadier William Segrave and Brigadier Cuthbert Martin were both awarded two DSOs for gallantry or meritorious service – at that time Britain's second-highest award below the Victoria Cross.

Beaumont's contribution to the Second World War was no less impressive, with eighty-seven OBs dying. Four were executed in German concentration camps and ten survived the Burma Railway as prisoners of war. The de Vomecourt brothers – Pierre, Jean, and Philippe – worked for the Special Operations Executive (SOE) and in 1941 set up the first resistance network in France. Dividing France between them, they organised industrial sabotage on large factories. When arrested and imprisoned, Phillip escaped from a civilian prison under a pseudonym, but the Gestapo starved Jean to death in a concentration camp. Pierre convinced his judge he was not a civilian but a POW and went to Colditz Castle where he met fellow OB Howard Gee. Gee was one of only two civilian prisoners in Colditz, sent there after various escape attempts. He was a British civilian volunteer who joined the Finnish Army during the Russo-Finnish War in Finland in 1940. Gee arrived in Oslo two hours after the Germans captured it and was arrested and treated as a POW.

Captain Brian Dominic Rafferty, Royal Berkshire Regiment, and Major John Sehmer MBE, Royal Tank Regiment, were attached to the SOE. Gestapo officers arrested Rafferty in France in February 1944 and imprisoned him at Dijon Prison where, brutally tortured, he concealed his identity for several weeks. When he was discovered, he was sent to Flossenburg concentration camp, where after days of starvation in the dark and solitary confinement, he was hanged on 29 March 1945.

In April 1943, Sehmer oversaw the SOE mission in support of the Royal Serbian Army in Yugoslavia. He was withdrawn in May 1944 in preparation for Operation Windproof and parachuted into Czechoslovakia in September 1944 and became head of the British

Above left: Pierre de Vomécourt.

Above right: Captain Brian Dominic Rafferty.

mission to the Slovak National Uprising. German soldiers captured Sehmer in late December 1944 and sent him to Mauthausen concentration camp in Austria, where in January 1945 SS officers executed him.

Bomber pilot Nicholas Tindal was shot down on 11 December 1940 over occupied France and imprisoned in Stalag Luft III, Poland. There he took part in the legendary Great Escape, forging documents of the escapees. He gave his place in the escape to a Polish airman whose wife was due to give birth in England. This airman was among those shot on the orders of Reichsmarschall Hermann Göring. Tindal attempted several escapes, once wearing a German uniform for eight days before being recaptured near Hamburg.

Among Berkshire's many splendid First World War memorials is the University of Reading's clock tower. Its designer was Herbert Maryon, a teacher at the then Reading College. In 1924, it was dedicated to staff and pupils who died during the First World War, and later to students and staff who died in the Second World War and in Afghanistan (2001–14). At 60 feet high, the brick tower has a clock, a bell, two individual wall-mounted plaques dedicated to graduates who died during the Afghanistan War and two rolls of honour devoted to staff and pupils who died during both world wars. Additionally, a red plaque honouring soldier, poet and former college student Wilfred Owen is on a wall close to the tower.

Reading University war memorial.

Inset: Plaque to Wilfred Owen.

Another clock memorial forms part of Leckhampstead village war memorial. Unusually, its minutes are marked by .303 bullets, its hours by .303 cartridges, and its clock hands are bayonets. It commemorates eighty-nine local men, seventeen of whom died, while serving during the First World War. It is enclosed by a chain salvaged from a ship that fought at the Battle of Jutland (31 May – 1 June 1916), held in place by twelve 4-inch shell cases mounted on low, pyramidal, posts.

Leckhampstead.

While it's not unusual to find several private memorials within churches, halls and schools in a town or village, it is unusual to have more than one public memorial. Datchet has three. The first is the London Road, a crucifix erected in 1919 as a wayside shrine to those who served in France. A year later, a large 9-foot-high, ornately carved, Cornish granite Celtic cross was erected in the churchyard of St Mary the Virgin, raised by the women of Datchet in memory of those from the parish who fell in the First World War. In the same year, the parish council built an octagonal cenotaph on the green, surmounted by an urn with a lion on its front face and flanked by draping laurel leaves. In 1989, the names of the men who died during the Second World War were added to the cenotaph, and in 2014 a war memorial bench called the 'Tommy Bench' was unveiled, remembering soldiers who fought in both world wars.

At Ascot, on a roundabout outside the racecourse on top of a 9-foot plinth of Portland stone, stands an 8-foot 6-inch-high equestrian statue of Poppy the warhorse. The monument is the first national memorial dedicated to the millions of UK, Commonwealth and Allied horses, mules and donkeys killed during the First World War. Poppy pays tribute to the nobility, courage, unyielding loyalty and immeasurable contribution animals played in giving us the freedom of today's democracy and signifies the last time the horse would be used on a mass scale in modern warfare.

Reading has a memorial to sixteen people connected to the town who died during the Spanish Civil War (1936–39). Originally unveiled in May 1990 in Dusseldorf Way, the 5-foot-high Portland stone sculpture of a woman with a deceased child commemorates the mothers of those killed during the war. At least sixteen people from Reading fought

Above left: Datchet's first First World War memorial.

Above right: Datchet's second First World War memorial.

Datchet's third First World War memorial.

WAR HORSE MEMORIAL
1914-1918

War horse monument, Ascot.

during the war as soldiers, medics or ambulance drivers. In Reading many people helped raise funds for refugees and sent food aid to Spain. It previously stood outside the old Civic Centre, now demolished. In 2015, it was moved, restored, and relocated to Forbury Gardens.

In 1939, the government requisitioned Littlecote House, Hungerford, for military use. Between 1942 and 1943 it was headquarters to United States 34th Army Tank Brigade, commanded by Brigadier J. Noel Tetley. In September 1943, the US 101st Airborne Division took over part of the house, as the headquarters company of 1st Battalion, 506th Parachute Infantry Regiment. Their commanding officer, Colonel Robert Sink, used the library as his office, and it now contains a memorial plaque.

The 101st Airborne Division took off during the night of 5/6 June 1944 from nearby airfields, including RAF Ramsbury, as part of the invasion of Normandy. The legendary Easy Company, 2nd Battalion, 506th Parachute Infantry Regiment commander Dick Winters was among their number, made famous by Stephen Ambrose's book and TV mini-series, *Band of Brothers*.

In the parkland estate at Hamstead Marshall is a stone and granite memorial to the memory of the men of 501st Parachute Infantry Regiment. Billeted there in the weeks leading up to D-Day, they returned briefly in August 1944 before taking part in Operation Market Garden and parachuting into the Netherlands on 7 September 1944.

Three slate memorial stones are at Greenham Common, site of the former USAAF airbase. The centre stone is dedicated to US servicemen who lost their lives during the Second World War Two. On either side stones mark the American servicemen killed in

Greenham Common, memorial.

two separate accidents days apart in 1944. The first, on 12 December 1944, involved a Horsa glider that killed thirty-three members of the 17th Airborne Division. The second, on 15 December, was a collision between two B-17 bombers, resulting in the deaths of sixteen members of 306th Bombardment Group.

Another aviation memorial exists at Carpenters Wood, Maidenhead. It is dedicated to the missing crew of the Royal Air Force's 578 Squadron, who died on the morning of 18 July 1944 while flying over Berkshire. Twenty-one Halifax bombers en route to Caen, France, from Burn, North Yorkshire, were flying over Berkshire when a fire broke out on board Halifax LK794 LK-Q (AKA Q for Queenie). Avoiding the heavily populated areas of Reading, Maidenhead and Windsor, the pilot, Australian Flying Officer Victor Starkoff, broke formation and flew over open country where at 05.20 the fully fuelled and armed aircraft exploded in mid-air over dense wood near Pinkney's Green. The rear gunner a Canadian, Flt Sgt Hugh Sloan, was blown out of his turret and parachuted to safety. The rest of the crew disappeared without a trace. Their names are recorded on panels of the Commonwealth Air Forces Memorial to the Missing at Runnymede.

Craters from the impact can still be seen. The original wooden memorial was erected in July 1998, but due to weather and damage was replaced by a more substantial tribute in October 2008. The site and memorial being cared for by the Maidenhead Air Training Corps.

Acknowledgements

In finding the primary sources needed to research and produce this publication I am thankful and indebted to the many wonderful and like-minded people who I have met along the way. Their help, guidance, generosity and support as always have proved invaluable.

I am thankful to the staff of Berkshires County Council Library Services, particularly at Berkshire Record Office, Bracknell Library, Eton College and Reading Central Library; the Berkshire Record Office; Ken Fostekew of the Museum of Berkshire Aviation; the staff of Maidenhead Heritage Centre; Reading Museum; Berkshire Yeomanry Museum; the Rifles Berkshire and Wiltshire Museum; Dr Hugh Pihlens, Hungerford Virtual Museum; Tony Roberts; Berkshire Family History Society; John Conyard, www.comitatus.net; Bernice T. wryngwyrmuk.org; Robin Brown; Mark Armstrong, www.roman.org.uk; John Chapman, Berkshire War Memorials, berkswm.org; and members of the Rushmoor Writers Group, without whom it would not have been possible to complete this project.

For allowing the use of their images I am obliged to Callum Cromwell (CC), Comitatus re-enactment Group, Harry Payne (HP), Hungerford Virtual Museum(HVM), Legio VIII Augusta MGV, National Army Museum (NAM),Roman Living History Society Noel Sylvestre (NS), Wryngwyrm Vikings Dark Age War Band historical re-enactment group, National Portrait Gallery (NPG), Reading Museum (RM), Julian Temple (JT), the Sealed Knot re-enactment group, Hungerford Virtual Museum (HVM), Museum of Berkshire Aviation (MoBA), National Archives and Records Administration (NARA), Pangbourne College (PC; PdWC), and The Rifles Museum (TRM). All other images are from the author's collection, in the public domain or believed free from copyright.

I offer a special thanks for their continued meritorious support of me to my wife Maria, for keeping me focussed and for allowing me to do what I love doing. To my brother Richard Dunsmore, a kindred soul, and his wife Rachael Dunsmore, my RF. To Julian Temple, aviation historian and fellow author, and finally to S. Thomson-Hillis and Cathrine Milne, two amazing and invaluable friends who see what I can't see. Thank you all.

I am also grateful to Amberley Publishing for their continued support and for making my ambitions a reality.

About the Author

Dean has had a lifelong interest in military history. Following his father, grandfather, and great-grandfather he joined the army at sixteen, serving with the Royal Army Ordnance Corps for eight years as a Supply Specialist and Physical Training Instructor in the UK, West Germany, and Falkland Islands, attaining the rank of corporal. Following this he joined Surrey Police, retiring as a detective chief inspector after twenty-six years of service.

A battlefield and historic sites guide in the UK and Europe, Dean is a member of the Battlefield Trust, Guild of Battlefield Guides, and the Western Front Association. When not guiding he undertakes local military history walks, talks and tours in a variety of settings covering a range of military subjects.

Dean is regularly invited to speak at national and international conferences about military history and acts as a consultant for the planning and delivery of the New Jersey State Association of Chiefs of Police annual European battlefield staff ride programme.

Preceded by Hampshire, Kent, Sussex and Farnborough, this is Dean's fifth book in Amberley's Military Heritage series, and work is already underway on *Dorset's Military Heritage*.